THE DANCE MAKERS

THE DANCE MAKERS

Conversations with American Choreographers

Elinor Rogosin

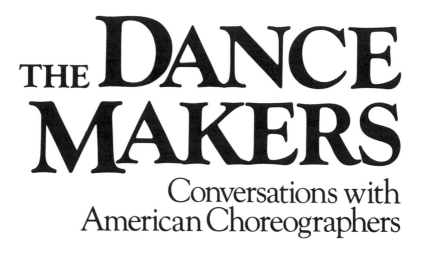

WALKER AND COMPANY
NEW YORK

Acknowledgments

I wish to thank the choreographers for participating in the original WBAI programs. I am especially grateful to those artists who generously agreed to update their activities for this book.

My thanks also to the many press, publicity, and administrative people who have helped arrange the interviews: particularly Meg Gordean on behalf of the Alvin Ailey American Dance Theatre; Cora Cahan of the Eliot Feld Ballet; and Tom Kerrigan, former press representative of the Martha Graham Dance Company.

And finally, my very special thanks to my editor, Ruth Cavin, for her cheerfulness and knowing support.

First published in the United States of America in 1980 by the Walker Publishing Company, Inc.

Published simultaneously in Canada by Beaverbooks, Limited, Don Mills, Ontario.

ISBN: 0-8027-0648-7

Library of Congress Catalog Card Number: 79-56003

Printed in the United States of America

Designed by Joyce Cameron Weston

10 9 8 7 6 5 4 3 2 1

Contents

Preface

SOME YEARS AGO, I produced a number of radio programs on dance for WBAI, an independent, nonprofit station affiliated with the Pacifica Foundation. "Dance Focus," as it was first called, occupied a half hour slot on alternate Saturday afternoons. Six months later, it formed a segment of a two-hour program called "For the Arts," and then it was switched back to a half-hour slot as "Dance Today." The fluctuation in programing greatly influenced the topics I covered as well as my choice of guests. I gave dance reviews during some seasons, and produced thematic series, such as discussions at the Brooklyn Academy of Music, during other seasons.

This book brings together a series of conversations with choreographers that were taped during my stay at WBAI. Since many of these conversations were held a number of years ago, I have updated the interviews to take into account events between the time of the original interview and the writing of this book. I have also added general background information on each choreographer, and bridges between these introductions and the actual interview. The tone of the introductions varies: in some instances, I am meeting the choreographer for the first time when we meet for the taping, and at other times I have a backlog of earlier experiences to call upon. Through these introductory memories and impressions, I have sought to reveal the common bond of courage which is an overlooked, but necessary, ingredient in the life of any choreographer. And I have chosen questions which bring out each choreographer's individual personality or aesthetic philosophy; I hope thereby to increase understanding of that artist's choreography in particular, and of the art of dance in general.

My choice of the twelve choreographers in this collection reflects my primary involvement with modern dance. Whenever I could, I planned programs that permitted me to meet its early pioneering figures, and the predominant theme of the conversations revolves around the establishment and growth of modern dance in America. Therefore, I have arranged the choreographers in an historical sequence to underline the story of modern dance as an art emerging from the dreams and efforts of a small, interlocked group of extraordinary people.

Because the last twenty years have seen a growing cross-fertilization between the worlds of modern dance and classical ballet, I have also included conversations with young American ballet choreographers who have been influenced by the interaction between the two worlds.

Elinor Rogosin

Remembering Ted "Papa" Shawn

The artist must be ecstatic about something.

My DRIVE THROUGH THE GREEN ROLLING HILLS of the Berk-shire mountains ended a short way past the town of Lee, Massachusetts, where a steep road off the highway brought me to Jacob's Pillow, the dance village I had come to visit. No one was visible at ten A.M. on a hot summer's morning, and except for the few cars that were parked in an open lot, I would have thought the place deserted. The quietness surprised me, as did the size of the parking area, for I had not expected any reminder of city life. Later, I learned that evening transformed the essentially serene atmosphere into a hectic scene of cars and people traveling up that steep hill to performances at the Ted Shawn Theatre. It was a telling reminder that Jacob's Pillow, as well as all the earlier dreams of Ted Shawn, had been both idealistic and practical.

Ever since I first heard the name Ted Shawn, I had been aware of Jacob's Pillow. Originally an old Massachusetts farm that Shawn and his group of male dancers transformed into a live-in summer dance school, Jacob's Pillow had been a seminal center for study and performing since the 1930's. It was not until 1970, however, that I visited "The Pillow," as it is commonly known, to record a segment for my radio program, "Dance Focus." Not only would the trip satisfy one of my oldest wishes, but the scheduled interview with Shawn loomed before me as a dramatic experi-ence. I would be meeting a man whom I knew only from the pages of dance books. A very unsettling thought, for, to me, Shawn was a living legend in the dance world; more myth than man. And since legends often have a power all their own, I didn't know whether I would be able to separate the man from the myth when I finally met this familiar stranger during my visit to his dance shrine.

On my arrival, I checked into the main office and then went over to the large studio barn where Barton Mumaw, an original member of Shawn's men's dance group in the 1930's, was teaching. I quietly climbed up a narrow flight of stairs to sit on a catwalk balcony to watch the class. In the airy classroom below, the young dance students followed Barton in a series of rhythmic swings. His directions, given in a soft southern voice, drifted up over pianist Jess Meeker's chords like an esoteric recitative: "Carriage of the arms in an arc through the air. . . . Now, let the entire torso follow through with the movement so that it doesn't stop within the head or the neck. . . . One, two, step, hold . . . And it moves in exact relationship to the amount of energy you're using. . . ."

I

The simplicity of the movements Barton was giving the class matched photographs of student dancers in classes at the Denishawn School in California. As I watched, I felt the clock had been turned back to the 1920's, to the early days of American dance. Those were days when a new, naturalistic form of organic dance was evolving out of the artistic vision of individuals like Ruth St. Denis and Ted Shawn.

When the class was over, I introduced myself to Barton and we went out to the garden to talk. Looking much younger than his sixty-odd years, he put his jacket on a large, smooth rock for me to sit on. We chatted about the early days of "The Pillow" and then I asked: "How did you come to dance with Ted Shawn? I don't think dancing was a popular career for a man when you were young."

Barton smiled. "I grew up in a small town in Florida, and the only two dancers, men dancers, that I really knew much about were Nijinsky and Ted Shawn. I had not seen them, just heard of them. When I did see Shawn, and that was the first time I had ever seen any dancing of that kind, the whole performance catalyzed me. It was like a spiritual awakening, and you know, that is part of the force of the artist. The next summer, I went to New York and studied at the Denishawn House there. I was with the last tour of Denishawn before the men dancers began, so I really go back to Denishawn."

As I had never seen the Denishawn Company on stage, I had to rely on pictures in dance books and on library reference material for a visual impression of its famous spectacles. In fact, this wasn't difficult—there must be hundreds of photographed moments, and even some film footage, picturing the extraordinary series of "living tableaux" that made up their repertoire. Costumes were incredibly ingenious and elaborate, the sets as outlandishly fantastic as in any 1930's Hollywood musical. An Egyptian pageant, an Algerian dream, a Babylonia reconstructed, a Crete imagined, an American Indian village reproduced; these were only a few of the extravagant exotic images that hypnotized the eye of the beholder during the 1920's when the Denishawn Company was at the height of its popularity.

I realized that during that period dance in America was an unchartered art; nevertheless, I was surprised by these obviously outlandish presentations. In addition, pictures of Shawn crouching low, with his feathered arms spread like the wings of a giant bird; slinking forward in a pair of harem pants slung low beneath a bare navel; lifting his arms in preparation for a Spanish flamenco step, made the work appear superficial, as though the dances were an excuse for the performers to dress up in ethnic cos-

A man touched by time and glowing with youthful enthusiasm for his love, the dance. Ted Shawn. (Courtesy of the Dance Collection, New York Public Library at Lincoln Center)

tumes. But this harsh critique was a result of looking back from the vantage point of a 1970's sophisticated dance art, a form whose early beginnings are to be found in these naive roots.

Behind the gaudy, theatrical Denishawn visions lay a serious search for authentic movement. From Ruth St. Denis had come an exploration of the spiritual aspect of life, and from Ted Shawn an understanding of the importance of gesture and emotions, influenced by the Delsarte system of movement. Their genius had been to combine their two personal visions into a form that was both original and exploratory, while enchanting audiences with beautiful dreams.

In 1933, after the Denishawn School and Company was dissolved, Shawn realized one of his life's dreams by forming a men's dance group. At that time, Americans had a very low opinion of men dancing, and an all-men's group was not only an innovative and dramatic way of focusing attention on men as dancers, but a very daring project. Its boldness overwhelmed me with amazement when I saw, from photographs and film clips, that Shawn's idea of marketing the concept of men dancing had been to put a group of half-naked men on stage in a variety of rhythmic, athletic poses glorifying virility. This is exactly what Shawn did, and with success, for his men's dance group became known and to a certain extent admired all over the country.

The Ted Shawn Dance Theatre at Jacob's Pillow was the first structure in the United States designed specifically for dance. Outside it resembles a barn, with the traditional weather vane replaced by a replica of Barton Mumaw in motion. Inside, a small stage and a steeply raked seating section provide very good sight lines. I was surprised by the life-sized paintings that dominate the theatre's foyer. On the right, Ruth St. Denis, eyes lowered, appears gentle and wise as Kwannon, the Japanese goddess of mercy. On the left, Ted Shawn, cloaked in feathers as a noble Indian, gazes into the distant vista. Together, their painted images overwhelm the theatre's rustic interior, transforming the entrance foyer into a shrine of dreams.

The afternoon's program opened with everyone singing "The Star Spangled Banner," a tradition that I hadn't encountered since my school days. Then Ted Shawn came out to make his Friday welcoming speech, a ritual that began in the 1930's, when curious neighbors were invited over to Jacob's Pillow for tea, a talk, and a demonstration of the company's work. His appearance on stage was the first time that I had seen the real Ted Shawn.

At first glance, dapper in a white suit and elegant in bearing, Shawn seemed younger than his age—seventy-eight. As he slowly walked towards the center of the stage, the audience waited silently, eagerly anticipating his first words. "I would like to welcome you to the sixth program of the thirty-eighth year of the Jacob's Pillow Dance Festival and the twenty-ninth year in this theatre. We have a rich, varied program of classi-cal ballet, American contemporary dance, and Hindu dance.''

His voice had a breathy quality, but the delivery was as assured and re-laxed as that of a seasoned actor playing a nightly performance. ''We wel-come back some old favorites. We welcome some exciting newcomers.'' A detailed explanation of the background of the dancers, and of the dances that each would perform, followed. His remarks made the printed program unnecessary, and after praising each of the performers he expanded: ''He [Lonny Joseph Gordon] expects and wants audience participation, and that means if he yells at you, and you feel like yelling back at him, you yell back at him. Now, this is similar to when we have Spanish dancing, be-cause it's right to scream and yell when you have a Spanish dancer on the stage. But this is definitely a trend nowadays, so if you are so inclined to participate, then let your conscience be your guide.''

The theatre was full, and the audience was delighted by Ted Shawn's short lecture, which came to its close with a disarming plea. ''On my bended knees . . . I'd need a derrick to get back up again . . . but I'll pretend I'm on my bended knees begging you to buy a souvenir program and patronize our book store, the proceeds of which go to our student scholarship fund.'' As Shawn left the stage, the audience responded with enthusiastic applause.

The curtain lifted for the Indian dancer, Bhasker, who launched the afternoon's program with an Indian fable. While I watched the perfor-mance, John Christian, Ted Shawn's friend and the general manager of ''The Pillow,'' silently came over to me. He cautioned, ''Shawn is ill and not too strong, so would you keep the interview short? We don't want to tire him.''

I followed Christian to a white frame house where we found Shawn in a comfortable high-back chair on his open porch. He had changed into an informal, one-piece jump suit and seemed to have dropped his role of impressario to assume the attitude of a gentleman farmer casually taking a midday rest. It was a perfect, clear summer day. The bright blue of the sky and the trees encircling us appeared to have been painted by a set designer to provide the proper background. I looked at Shawn as we were intro-duced, wondering to myself, where is the Ted Shawn of all those photo-graphs?

But there in front of me was the real Shawn, a man touched by time and glowing with youthful enthusiasm for his love, the dance. He remained seated during our interview, but the rhythms of his voice suggested an earlier vigor. As he talked, it occurred to me that instead of picturing him as he must have been, a hard-working dancer with a penchant for philosophizing, I had imagined a fantasy character: The pivotal figure in those dance books had become like a fictional character who inhabits the half-imagined reality of a long novel. And like such a character, he had gone on for years, wandering in and out of his own creation, the American dance.

But it was the image of Shawn as I'd actually seen him, sitting on his open porch in the gentle Berkshire hills, that came to me in 1972 when I heard that he had died.

e.r. Mr. Shawn, you've been famous for many years as an innovative American dancer and choreographer, as the founder of the Jacob's Pillow School and Festival, and perhaps most uniquely, for your pioneering efforts in establishing dance as a viable career for men. Do you think that people today, here in America, are more ready to accept a male dancer than they were when you first pioneered?

t.s. Oh, a thousand times more. The evidence is in the numbers of men all over the country who are earning their living entirely by dancing; it runs into thousands. Plus, some time ago when you looked at the different dance companies, it seemed to be a matriarchy, and now that is turned upside down. Except for Martha Graham, just name your top companies, Paul Taylor, Merce Cunningham, Alvin Ailey, Donald McKayle . . . Go down the line, they're all headed by men, and also every one of the ballet companies now has a fine contingent of male dancers. That was nonexistent when I began to campaign for male dancers with my company in 1933. We'd dance every chance we could, regardless of money. We would dance for a ten A.M. assembly program in a high school; anything to get at the boys in their formative years, to let them see what "right" dancing for men is, the kind of dancing that men have done throughout the ages. I came along, and then Gene Kelly. He did a wonderful show, *Dancing Is A Man's Game*, and I thanked him for it. I said, "You're helping in a cause that I've given my life to," and he said, "You're telling me? You and your men dancers came to my high school in Pittsburgh and that started me being a dancer." So you see, with one generation their minds have been changed, and then you have fine examples of male dancers for more young men to see. Now, I think the battle's completely won. I doubt that there's a living, intelligent human being who still thinks of dancing as a sissy profession.

e.r. No, things have changed, and everyone has a lot to thank you for. I'm very fond of Indian dance, and I was just watching that part of this afternoon's program before I came over here.

t.s. I, too, like the Indian dance very much. Here at Jacob's Pillow, we've presented many wonderful Indian dancers, including India's Balaraswati. We've had Ram Gopal, who came over several times

"Dancers must speak many languages and speak them fluently." Ted Shawn and Ruth St. Denis in Balinese Fantasy *(Photo: Nickolas Muray)*

from London, and we've also had many dancers who are not Hindu by birth or blood, but who, like La Meri and some of La Meri's pupils, are fine exponents of Hindu styles, and of course Matteo, and on down the line. I don't think there's ever been a season that we haven't had at least some true figure of Hindu dance on the program. Also, it has always been taught in our school.

e.r. *But isn't that part of your feeling and your philosophy about dance? That you believe in having dance from the entire world here at Jacob's Pillow?*

t.s. I've been fighting for that for nearly sixty years now, since I began to teach. I believe that dance isn't, "I'm a ballet dancer," . . . "I'm a modern dancer," . . . "I'm a Spanish dancer," and "I'll have no part of your dancing." It's almost like separate religious sects. I said, "Dance is dance, and we have to prepare total dancers." Dancers must speak many languages and speak them fluently, as an educated person masters French, or German, or Spanish, or even Chinese, nowadays. Today, just look at the things that ballet companies expect of dancers. Just recently, soloists from Montreal's Les Grands Ballets Canadiens were here, and on one of their programs, not a single person got on pointe. It could have been called a modern dance program.

e.r. *There's much more of a blend in today's dance.*

t.s. Such a blend, and it's wonderful. I like it. Again, I say that every dancer should have a sound knowledge of the two major ethnic techniques, that is, Hindu and Spanish, and also folk. I think there should be real feeling in folk dance, especially with our own background of American folk dance; the true American folk, not the hoked up, corny, quaint stuff. I mean dances like the quadrilles, and the long-ways dances, and the Caucasian circle and the classic forms of our early American dances.

e.r. *Are all those techniques taught here during the summer?*

t.s. We group together basic classical ballet and American contemporary modern dance. Then we group the others under the overall heading of ethnic dance. This summer we've already had Ritha Devi from India, who taught Indian dance for two weeks. Manila Vargas, who is a very fine Spanish dancer, is teaching now, and when he finishes, we'll have three separate courses. One will be in American folk dance. Then we'll have what my pupil, Jack Cole, calls "American urban folk," avoiding the word "jazz," and Dick Crowley will be teaching that; actually it's theatre dance. Then we will end the summer with a course taught by Jean Leon Destiné, who'll be giving a week of Haitian dance. Altogether, it gives our students a rich movement experience. Of course, one week will not train you to be a Haitian dancer, but it will give you some feel for it; so that, for instance, if you get a job and suddenly they decide to have a Caribbean scene and the choreographer has to work in that medium, you don't have to be frightened because you've had no experience with it. You'll have a richer palette of colors to paint from.

e.r.   *I would think so. Do you have a favorite dancer, or choreographer, or company working today? Am I putting you on the spot?*

t.s.   I love so many of them. That's the thing. I love all of dance, provided it's motivated by dedication and sincerity, and disciplined. Sometimes you'll have a dancer who has a rich emotional content but hasn't accepted the discipline of communication in an art form. Then other people who are technically fabulous, but you feel a coldness or an emptiness of content. But, oh, I love so many dancers.

e.r.   *Then when the technique and the emotion come together in beauty . . . ?*

t.s.   So often, I quote five words from Ouspenski: ``Art is the communication of ecstasy.`` Those words are very important. The artist must be ecstatic about something; he burns at a brighter flame, he vibrates at a higher level of intensity. And he must feel that what he's got is something he must share with you. It is so beautiful, so wonderful, that he can't keep it to himself. He's got to share it with you. Then if he has disciplined himself to such an extent that he can communicate, and through empathy you also become ecstatic, and share this beauty with him, and go away with something that is permanently added to your life, then, I think, you have the art of the dance. It can come through many forms. Also, there are those magic performances that hit you unexpectedly. Three or four or five times in my whole lifetime, at totally unexpected moments, something has been so magically perfect, so ecstatic on such a tremendous level and power, that I have sat in the theatre and just cried my heart out. And it's that magic that keeps you going. You put up with good performances. You sit there, you feel the back of your seat and you open your program and you read. The curtain goes up; you say, ``Beautiful, lovely body, nice, clean technique.`` You clap politely. But then, if at some moment, and you never know until afterwards, you're pulled away from the back of your chair, that very word, *ekstas*, meaning that you stand outside of yourself describes the experience you're having. Only when it's over do you realize that you're in the theatre, and you feel the back of your seat again. That's worth putting up with a hundred mediocre performances, because if you don't go, you might miss that one.

A Visit to Charles Weidman

It's a scale built from space.

During the 1960's, Charles Weidman established what turned out to be his last school of dance in a small, narrow loft located on Twenty-ninth Street, at the edge of Manhattan's garment center. A new generation of students met Charles in one or another of his guest-teaching assignments around the country, and then, when they could, came to study with him in this studio. From these young, loyal dance students, he formed the Theatre Dance Company, which performed his classics every Sunday night in the Expression of Two Arts Theatre, as the loft was called on the occasions when it became a theatre.

For years, until Charles's death in July 1975, I was sure of seeing the Expression of Two Arts Theatre's program listed in Section Two of the Sunday *New York Times* under the day's dance events. Some weeks, it was almost the only Sunday evening dance listing, while at other times it was lost in the crowded schedule of dance performances. As the programing always included the name of Weidman's famous works, such as *The Unicorn in the Garden* (after James Thurber's story) or *Traditions*, it was apparent that a visit to his theatre was essentially a trip into the past.

I finally traveled down to the Expression of Two Arts Theatre on a cold April evening about three years before Charles's death closed it forever. I climbed the dingy flight of stairs to the first landing, where I stopped before a blue door marked "Charles Weidman School of Dance." As I opened the door and entered the loft, I was surprised to see that most of the audience had arrived even earlier than I.

These early arrivals were already waiting in the odd assortment of chairs and stools that had been placed in a jagged, horizontal line near the audience. By arranging the seats in this pattern, a long, narrow section of the old, sparsely furnished loft was left open as a performing space. On subsequent visits I saw other seating arrangements, designed to change the depth of the performing area, but never were there more than about twenty people in the audience; otherwise, there would have been little or no room for the dancers to dance.

I hung up my coat in a corner coatrack and looked around for an empty chair. Since most of the seats were occupied, I realized that those already

"There is that magical thing of the body moving." The young Charles Weidman (Courtesy of the Dance Collection, New York Public Library at Lincoln Center)

10

settled in must be frequent visitors to the loft—part of Weidman's faithful following. I eventually discovered that, although the earliest comers naturally had first choice, people were always extremely polite about taking either the most comfortable of the unreserved seats, or those in the front row.

"Oh, no, you take that one."

"I'll just sit here, thank you."

"We're two."

It might have been indecision about which actually were the best seats in a space too small to gain the ordinary illusion of theatrical perspective, but participation in this weekly seating became a ritual introduction to the theatre's spartan atmosphere. The experience of choosing a chair at the Expression of Two Arts Theatre had as much to do with integrity as being able to see the dancing. For essentially, everyone involved had come to sit at a shrine of memory, and no one ever rushes to the first row of any church.

There was always a core of older women at these Sunday evenings who looked as if they might have been students at one of Charles's earlier schools. Usually a group of younger dancers was present as well, and I particularly admired their appearance at an unfashionable concert, at a time when New York was overflowing with all types of new dance. Everyone who came to the loft for these performances was unusually friendly, and there were a great many nods and smiles as people recognized one another from a previous Sunday, an old dance class, or other concerts. We all understood the basis of our silent camaraderie, however. No one ever stated it out loud, yet it was clear. The Sunday audiences at the Expression of Two Arts Theatre were in attendance to honor Charles Weidman, and to keep him from being forgotten.

I was curious but not very bold on my first visit to the theatre, and I took a seat in the second row, hoping that it would give me some feeling of perspective. Looking straight ahead into the performing space, I saw that the windows and the right side of the room had been curtained off in an effort to block the light coming in from the street. In addition to making the area something of a designed stage set, the curtains also had a practical function, keeping technical equipment from sight and giving the dancers a place from which they could enter and exit, change costumes, and take a moment's rest. At the very back of the loft, directly behind our chairs, were the usual studio desk and bulletin boards. To the side of the desk was a door, and through that door was the room where Charles Weidman lived.

Shortly after seven-thirty, with the audience settled in and no room left for late arrivals, Weidman came shuffling out from his living quarters. He was, I saw, a tall, gaunt, black-haired man wearing glasses and dressed in loose pants and ballet slippers. In his seventies at the time, Weidman bore only a slight resemblance to the well-known photographs of himself as a young dancer. The smooth freshness in the face of the youth had been overrun by a mass of lines and wrinkles, which not only affected his individual features but controlled the outward look with which he met our inquisitive glances. A vivacious energy still lingered on his sensitive face, but it was off-key. Those varied expressions that constantly float across our eyes and smiles had been lost in the process of aging, and the essence of his personality had been frozen into a fixed gaze of wonder.

Speaking in broken spurts, stopping and starting as though jumping over a pulsating nerve carelessly exposed, Weidman welcomed us. The short speech he gave to introduce the evening's program quickly became a humorous, deprecating comment on the evening's dances, beginning with *Easter Oratorio*, his own deeply felt work set to the awesome music of Bach. "The expression of the joy of the resurrection is the overwhelming mood in the piece. Now there are six sections. In the first, there is this angel who is over there in that corner, and. . . .

"Then we'll do *Traditions*, a piece I did way back when. . . .

"*Kinetic Pantomime*, for which I'm known, or so they say. . . .

"One of my students has choreographed *Rhumba to the Moon*, and that'll be our light dance tonight. . . .

"We'll end with *Brahms Waltzes, Opus 39*, which I dedicated to Doris [Humphrey] because it is the kind of movement she loved and could dance so beautifully."

The Theatre Dance Company, a group of nine young people, entered the performing space and *Easter Oratorio* began. I was touched by the ardor of spiritual faith in the piece and felt that I could have been eavesdropping on someone at prayer, it was so personal. Choreographically, too, there was an apparent simplicity, emphasizing open, bold movements. One such movement, a clean gesture of fully extended arms, hands with palms up, was very strong and became more and more effective each time it was repeated. Feats of skill were of little importance, and perhaps it was this lack of acrobatic virtuosity in their work that created such a refreshing impact of naive expression. The young dancers, girls and boys, projected an air of devotion not only in this piece, but in all their dancing during the evening.

Then Charles, enveloped in a piece of fabric, danced *Submerged Cathedral*, his impression of a visionary scene. Using the large covering cloth, which gave an angular, sculptured look to the movements of his body, he created the feeling of a rising and falling structure, while in the background the drifting, emotional music of Debussy filled out this subtle interpretation of a Brittany legend.

At first, Charles's skeletal face with its half-closed, inwardly focused eyes, was the only part of his body left uncovered. Later, at the close of the dance, when he withered forever into the folds of fabric, his head, like the uppermost tip of a sinking cathedral tower, slowly disappeared as well.

Charles's intense absorption and concentration throughout transformed the simple movements into a poetic sensation. His performance in this unusual, almost mystical, piece brought a strong dramatic element into the evening's effort. Although he was seventy-two and no longer had the physical strength to leap or perform other acts of demanding agility, Charles's dancing still had vestiges of articulate, graceful movement, and his elegant artistry was still intact. Watching Charles Weidman perform, it was clear that his talent was the pivotal, guiding force of the young Theatre Dance Company, which honored him with its impassioned dancing of the evening's final piece, *Brahms Waltzes, Opus 39.*

The evening came to an end with the same simplicity of spirit with which it had begun. After the last piece the young dancers, hand in hand and with the joyfulness of love shining on their faces, bowed to the appreciative audience. When Charles came forward, the audience stood in respect, hoping that its enthusiastic applause would return some of the warmth it had received during that evening's defiant effort.

Shortly after my introductory visit to a Sunday night concert at the Expression of Two Arts Theatre, I arranged to interview Charles for a WBAI program. He was preparing the company for a performance at the Ninety-Second-Street Young Men's Hebrew Association, a New York stronghold of modern dance for over thirty years, and welcomed the opportunity to publicize the concert. I was interested in discussing *Submerged Cathedral*, and so we made an arrangement to meet at his loft. I found him to be a very friendly, loquacious man and an interesting person to interview, though he stuttered, making it difficult to edit the tape for airing.

In December 1974, I contacted Charles again. This time I was preparing an article for *Eddy*, a small dance magazine. I had been impressed by Charles's courage and wanted others to be aware of him as a person. I knew that behind his humorous facade was a dramatic history of ups and downs that could easily have undone the strongest personality. He had been through artistic and financial success and failure, and through bouts of alcoholism. He had been pushed aside while others used his pioneering work to further their own careers. But Charles not only survived, he prevailed, and with little available in the way of resources, he maintained both his school and his company for over twenty years.

We made an appointment for a day in mid-December. When I arrived at the Expression of Two Arts Theatre, we went into his little room off the back of the one-room studio-*cum*-school-*cum*-theatre. He had a cold and was sniffling and mentioned that his back had been giving him some trouble. I was shocked that there was no heat source other than a small electric heater, which took the chill out of the air but certainly left the room far from warm. Charles could not have been feeling all that well, yet not only did he sit and reminisce about his life, but when we finished talking, he started a rehearsal with the young members of his company.

Charles's enthusiasm, though he guarded it with a mocking eye, was undauntable. That and sheer guts kept him going right through the hardship of a cold winter. He was still giving the Sunday night concerts when he died, the following July, a few days short of his seventy-fourth birthday.

The conversation that follows is an intercut of the 1972 and 1974 interviews.

e.r. Mr. Weidman, whenever I've seen you perform, I've been fascinated by your concentration and intensity. I was particularly impressed by your performance in Submerged Cathedral, *which I saw you dance two years ago, and now again in Bach's* Easter Oratorio. *You seem to be transformed from a person who is dancing or performing into the thing itself. Are you aware of a special something happening? Do you know what is in your mind at the time, or how it comes about?*

c.w. No. Through all these many years I have either trained myself, or developed a technique, of translating a certain feeling about either a section of music or an idea which I as an interpreter am conveying to the onlooker. That's my job. I would say as a good interpreter, my dance should give you *that* same feeling which I feel that a particular piece of music or an idea is expressing at *that time*.

e.r. It's a reaction, then. You're really connected to the music.

c.w. The music, that's first. In Debussy's *Submerged Cathedral*, a man is dancing it, so, therefore, at the very end, the way the cloth comes over the face is like the sea coming over a man. The man becoming the cathedral, that idea. In *Easter Oratorio*, it is a tormented soul who is helped eventually by that angel up there, even though the angel has some doubts because of the echo who is telling the angel, "No, or yes." So that's a personalized kind of dramatic abstraction.

e.r. It all comes through your feelings.

c.w. The feelings, yes.

e.r. I read that you were born in Nebraska and left there to study dance at Denishawn in California. How had you heard of Denishawn?

c.w. I was artistically inclined at a very early age and thought I would become an architect. I had had folk dance in my grade school, and I didn't care so much for that. Later on, Irene and Vernon Castle were in vogue, and their lovely sweeping movements fascinated me. I liked their kind of dance. However, I didn't think of dance as a career. Then my interest in architecture developed into a curiosity about the history of architecture, and I read about the Hanging Gardens of Babylon, and about Greece, and Egypt. I was so involved with that kind of thing, at times I thought I'd give up architecture and become an archeologist or historian. Then Ruth St. Denis came to the Orpheum Theatre in Lincoln, Nebraska, with her pageant of India, Egypt, and Greece, and there was my history, dancing before me. I just put two and two together, and from then on I wanted to do that kind of dancing.

e.r. *So you discovered Denishawn because the company was touring the country. There's been a lot of touring in modern dance. I think part of dance being one of today's fastest-growing arts must be due to groundwork laid by all that touring.*

c.w. I should say so. I'm still doing it. Last week I went up to the University of Calgary in Canada. That was the two hundred and fourth college in which I've taught.

e.r. *And are the students really interested in learning dance?*

c.w. Yes. On Tuesdays, I go down to the University of Maryland where they're putting on a repertory work of mine, *The War between Men and Women* [after James Thurber's stories], but they have their own dance department. They fought a long time for it. When the schools do get the dance majors, the whole standard is lifted and the students can achieve more.

e.r. *Back to the days when you were traveling with the Denishawn Company, did its 1925 tour of the Orient have an effect on you, on your working?*

c.w. Oh, surely, especially at that time. When we went to Japan, there were many cities where we were the first foreign troupe to appear. It was very thrilling for us at that time, and for them, too. We interpreted those oriental things with Denishawn. The Japanese were especially wonderful audiences. In Japan, though, we didn't do many of the Japanese dances, because, naturally, they did them so much better. So coming back from that tour, we decided to forget all about that Oriental stuff. We revolted against that form of dancing: dancing Japanese, Chinese, Javanese, Singhalese, Spanish, all that, and against the ballet. Instead, we thought, why not evolve a form of dance which is indigenous to this country? Rough though it may be, we could take it all over the world and say, this is America dancing. Now Isadora Duncan had believed that too, but she had done nothing, that I know about, for men. Her dance was very beautiful, personal, and feminine. Also, we were very conscious of our social commitment because Hitler had come onto the scene. We thought that we as artists should do something about it. There were many dances against war and injustice and things like that, so to go on dancing in an oriental sari or something like that, no; it was out of place. We wanted to do something that would be of the world today, modern. Modern, that was the whole idea.

e.r. *It was a very strong idea; look where it's gone. At that time, did you envision it would ever be popular?*

c.w. No. We didn't realize it then. We just wanted to do what we had in mind. Another very strong thought at the time was to elevate the dance from being mere entertainment, from dancing like the Rockettes, and things like that. We wanted to lift the dance to a level similar to that achieved by the other arts.

e.r. *I've read that while in Japan, you worked with Kabuki dancers. Did that have any effect on your personal style?*

c.w. I learned a role that was purely Japanese, and most of my solo was based on percussive things, done with my knees on the stage, like a drum. That affected my modern feeling. Much of modern dance has been on that lower level, and a lot of people were affected with that whole scale of dance. By scale, I mean if I stood up, I would be in what I would call that norm. Then there's the air, and also the floor, so you have a scale which a dancer moves through; it's a scale built from space.

e.r. *I think that part of the early success of modern dance came from your talent as a performer as well as from your theories. I've never seen Doris Humphrey dance, but I understand she was a very lyrical dancer. Is that so?*

c.w. She was very beautiful that way. Yes, especially lyrical when she danced with the Denishawn Company. Later, as a modern dancer, she developed very dramatic parts. She danced the matriarch in her own *With My Red Fires*, and then she was Theda Bara in my *Flickers*. Just very broadly speaking, Martha [Graham] was more or less almost always more on the earth, but Doris was always up, up, up; and she was very lovely and lyrical.

e.r. *And also in temperament?*

c.w. Yes, but Doris was a very strong thinker, as much so as Martha. However, she liked Helen [Tamiris] very much because Tamiris was very straightforward; but she didn't agree with Martha too much, because Martha said, "I feel," instead of "I think." Doris used her head a great deal.

e.r. *You were telling me before about your part in a program on the roots of American dance, but for you it isn't a subject to study, it's your life. First came Denishawn, and then modern dance developed from a few ex-Denishawn dancers, and you were one of them.*

c.w. Our leaving Denishawn was very unhappy in so many ways, and against so many of our ideas or ideals. I had more or less to close my eyes to much. I was always very fond of Miss Ruth, and in her biography she says that she was very fond of me, too. All the Denishawn traveling was by train and I spent hours on the train with her. I helped her tidy her big religious dramas, and things like that. I was always very good at listening to her. Then finally, when it came to founding the New York Denishawn House at Van Cortland Park, they only invited Doris to teach. There was a lot of misunderstanding at that time. Also, the company had to be 90 percent Aryan. We had just done our concert at the Guild, where 75 percent or 80 percent of the girls were Jewish, so that didn't make sense and it wasn't right. It was upsetting; some things you don't want to think about. The separation from Denishawn was like that. So you forget about all the love you had. It's like the World War. The Japanese were wonderful to us when we were there, but then we had a war and we're supposed to hate the Japanese; I just couldn't. You say to yourself, "That's war," but they had been too kind to us. Eventually, with Miss Ruth, too. I forgot all about the ending of our association, and closed my eyes to all the things that were so uncomfortable. I made it a point, every time I was out on the West Coast, to look her up and do things with her.

e.r. *You mean later, in the years after.*

c.w. After, yes.

e.r. *When you and Doris Humphrey first started to do your own concerts, audiences must have been very different from what they are today. How did you go about things then? There weren't any grants.*

c.w. We did everything on our own. Doris and I became popular and very successful. When we did our concert at the Gallery Theatre, I heard that Miss Ruth had come there.

e.r. *You were pioneering, for dance, for audiences.*

c.w. There was a great interest in modern music. I remember a Mrs. Max Walden, who was a very wonderful person. She opened her apartment to composers for sessions in which they came and talked, and she served coffee and sandwiches. Lehman Engel and all those composers came, and they wrote music for us. Doris and I were also on the Washington Irving High School concerts, and the students loved our kind of dance, so, eventually we built an audience. The modern dance grew with the help of the Bennington College people. Then many colleges put dance into their programs and that developed students and concerts.

e.r. *That was the base, and then it took off. Do you find it difficult, so many years later, to revise works from the Humphrey-Weidman Company?*

c.w. Yes. I'm reviving one of Doris's early pieces now. I had tried to get the phrasing, and it was difficult to remember exactly. When we finally got the music, it helped, because there was always a recurring five-four beat: four and one, two, and three, four, five, and one, two, three, four, two, two, three. . . . I remember that feel, and we finally got more of it when we saw the movie of *New Dance* that was taken

Charles Weidman in A House Divided *(Courtesy of the Dance Collection, New York Public Library at Lincoln Center)*

on the lawn up at Bennington. I've done an opening. It's just the spirit. We'll just have to let it go at that, unless someone can contradict me and can come in and contribute something more, especially if there's enough interest for someone to do it in his or her own company.

e.r.   *Are there other works of yours or of Doris Humphrey's that have been filmed?*

c.w.   I'm hoping to get several things filmed. At New London [Connecticut College Summer Dance Session] they did film *Bargain Counter*. I'm not too pleased with the *Lynchtown*, though I've signed a release contract for it with the Dance Notation Bureau. They have a videotape machine over there, and they may videotape the whole program that I'm working on now, or they may just do *Traditions*.

e.r.   *Do you give a lot of your pieces to different companies?*

c.w.   I've done quite a bit of that, yes. Most of the companies have asked for the piece I dedicated to Doris Humphrey, *The Brahms Waltzes*, which owes a lot to her idea of movement. It was done more or less as a memorial to Doris, like the St. Denis piece that I did for Miss Ruth. I dedicated the *Waltzes* to Doris because it used a lot of her main technique, which was based on fall and recovery. Martha Graham's technique was based on contraction and release. So those big falls toward the end of the piece [*Brahms Waltzes*] are Doris's first series of falls, and they're done more dramatically than the music. There are more suspensions, and the suspension in movement is like an earmark of what they call Humphrey-Weidman technique. The suspension is a very important quality in our work.

e.r.   *Was that use of fall and recovery, or suspension, one of the differences between early modern dance and ballet?*

c.w.   It's a strange word to use, but our lyricism has more weight. It's related to the gravity pull and it has more weight than ballet. In ballet, they go up so beautifully and defy gravity, but we have more drama in the pull against gravity; it's extended, like the breath.

e.r.   *You're also known for your kinetic pantomime. What exactly is it?*

c.w.   Kinetic pantomime is a sort of revolt against representational pantomime. It's more or less like abstract music. You can go into more abstractions than if you are pinned down by doing certain things to tell your story clearly. I do both, and each has a different result.

e.r.   *And what you call representational tells more of a story?*

c.w.   It's all storytelling. Yes, representational pantomime generally tells a story. Kinetic pantomime takes the movement value or design value of a certain pantomimic gesture and expands upon it. Of course, the sky's the limit with a technique like that. Actually, kinetic pantomime developed from a duet I did with Agnes De Mille. Way back, at the beginning, I guess that I was kind of rare; by rare, I mean there were very few modern dancers, men dancers around New York and available for programs or concerts. I did some concerts, and Agnes wanted me to do one with her, which I did. We danced *May Day*, a sort of Bavarian boy-and-girl number in which they go out and have a picnic. There's a great big basket, and a tablecloth on the ground, and pickles, and salami, and cheese and crackers. I said, ''This has got to go.'' I thought, if only the pantomime were not so literal. Even with Denishawn, or even with my first solo, a scherzo, *Troubador*, I worked with imaginary props. I was used to things being imaginary, but this was not, and I had such a violent reaction against it that I decided to do something about it. After I started working with kinetic pantomime, I went up to Bennington during the summer. I forget what year that was. I thought I would try to expand my work into a group composition, and that developed into *Opus 51*, I call it *Commedia*. It's supposed to look quite improvisational, like the early commedia dell'arte, but it has no rhyme nor reason. In a comedy piece, I completely cut off the theme and go into something else, and that makes it have more of a sparkle.

e.r. *That fits your satiric sense of things. When you look around at the world today, what do you think?*

c.w. I get very disgusted with a lot of things. I sort of crawl up in my ivory tower, here in my Twenty-Ninth-Street loft, in front of my electric heater, and just go on.

e.r. *Are you working on a special project now?*

c.w. Mary Anthony has arranged a grant for me from the National Endowment to do my version of Thurber's *Fables for Our Times*. I'll revive *The Unicorn in the Garden*, *The Owl Who Was God*, and *The Shrike and the Chipmunk*. Mary has also asked me to guest with her company and to give workshops. I give a two-hour lesson in technique and idea. I give them a semblance of kinetic pantomime as well.

e.r. *Didn't you and Doris Humphrey have a school?*

c.w. Yes, and a studio theatre on Sixteenth Street.

e.r. *At that time, what did you look for in a dancer?*

c.w. You have an idea, or you want to do a ballet, and then you choose your people. For instance, the first full-length ballet that I did in the modern idiom was Beerbohm's *The Happy Hypocrite*. I didn't have enough men to do the parts, but I was always fond of Eleanor King for her pantomime, so she was the first Mr. Aeneas, the mask-maker. Later, José [Limon] came and did the part. So, it all depends upon how well people do things. You give them the opportunity to try them. Here, because we're dancing almost every Sunday night through the year, my dancers have a very good chance of interpreting and learning different parts.

e.r. *I would imagine with so many years of teaching, that your eye is trained to spot what can be done with a dancer; what's there in personality.*

c.w. Surely, yes. My eye, after all these years, good Lord!

e.r. *And when you yourself work, do you usually start from an idea or from music?*

c.w. I like music. I don't like electronic music, though. It puts me to sleep, really, it has that sort of effect on me. I'd rather have the dance without the music. I don't know why modern dancers don't use better music. I know a great deal about music, because I've gone through so much of it. In the very beginning, many of our scores were created for us by very good composers. But lately, I've been having a jag on *Madame Butterfly*. That's a gorgeous score. I had to tackle the *Fables* [Thurber's *Fables for Our Time*] on Thanksgiving Day, and I was working on some very graphic sections that I didn't even remember. I spent five hours doing that, but I couldn't take too much of Frieda Miller [music and piano for *Fables*], so I'd come back in here and put on Puccini's gorgeous *Madame Butterfly*, and then go back and tackle Frieda Miller some more.

e.r. *You worked on Broadway at one time. Did you like it?*

c.w. Yes. I enjoyed it, but I didn't like the pressure. Many times I had to stay up all night working out things for the next day's rehearsal. I wouldn't work under such pressure any more.

e.r. *Is the time more your own when you're doing concert dance?*

c.w. You make it your own.

e.r. *Do you feel that you're a living monument?*

c.w. No, I don't.

e.r. *I mean, when you pick up a book, there you are, in the pages.*

c.w. I'm supposed to be a myth in Australia. I've a whole big library that I haven't ever read. It's over there. I've got to drag out my notes for this revival I'm doing with the company when they come tonight. That takes a lot of my time, and the Mary Anthony Company has taken an awful lot of time. We haven't done these fables since 1949. I have two records of *The Owl Who Was God* and *Charlie the Chipmunk*. They're awful records, but the music is pretty much as I remember it. Frieda Miller, the pianist, loved these scores, and she loved the *Fables*, and so she made a note that no one else was going to play it but her. Thank God for these records, because the work is not set down anywhere, and the actual written score is nothing like what we did. I had to do all that digging out, how many measures of this, and what repeats, and that was difficult. I was trying to feel around, and what did I have: a secretary bird, a dormouse, ground moles, a rock hen, a French poodle, and a hawk. So I said to the dancers, "You come in and just improvise."

e.r. *You had to direct them?*

c.w. Yes.

e.r. *Is that what keeps you so full of energy?*

c.w. I'm consumed. It just consumes me.

e.r. *I think you thrive on it.*

c.w. Well, I've a bad back.

e.r. *It seems to me that you are full of enthusiasm for your work.*

c.w. You've got to keep that. That's like an actor who assumes a part, any part. You may feel tired, but you've got to pull yourself up to the right pitch.

e.r. *How do you do that?*

c.w. That's a talent, too.

e.r. *Can you learn it?*

c.w. I don't know. We had a very vicious training with Denishawn. All those years of tours. You'd just collapse at the end after three or four months. No one got sick. You couldn't get sick. If you were sick and if you were in bed, but could get up and walk, then you danced. If you fell back, you couldn't dance. That was the training.

e.r. *Certainly no coddling.*

c.w. We had no understudies.

e.r. *It went into your systems.*

c.w. Into your hearts, yes. I do know that a lot of what is said in Mabel Todd's book, *The Thinking Body*, does happen. For example, fatigue can bring on false energy. I remember many times during Denishawn when I was putting on makeup before a performance, I didn't know how I was going to get through. I was so tired, but finally, I got up on stage and danced. It's sort of a false energy. Something happens. It's magic in the whole body and it's from the mind. That's a statement by Mabel Todd, who is an authority on things like that.

e.r. *Dance is connected to feelings, isn't it?*

c.w. There is that magical thing of the body moving. Many times you might have a cold or something and feel lousy, but after you dance a little bit and sweat, you feel much better. It's getting into the body. The dance makes you do that, otherwise, you think; "I won't get out." You won't do it unless you have an inner something to do it for . . .

e.r. *Is that the magic secret, the thing that made you start and keeps you going?*

c.w. You find that true of almost every artist, I would say, that inner desire.

e.r. *And that's a desire to dance, to create, to express?*

c.w. To express, I would say. All those things. The dance and the thing to give. To give, when you stop that, then you retire.

e.r. *That's it. You never lost that ability, that desire to give.*

c.w. At times it's very hard. Sometimes I feel sort of low, maybe because of an ailment or something like that. I can get depressed. And well, I always felt a person should be like a spring, like a coil. When you do get low down, then in the technique we have something that is quite awful, quite wonderful; it is the ability to rebound, to shift energy from a fall into action. Rebound is in the technique and in the attitude. To rebound and then to start all over again.

Conversation with Martha Graham

Whatever one dances, one is.

I T IS JUST BEFORE NOON on a Saturday morning in 1948. We are ten teen-age girls, members of the Saturday class for young people at the Martha Graham School of Contemporary Dance, and this Saturday, as usual, my classmates and I are leaning on the ballet barre while listening to our teacher, Erick Hawkins. He stands before us, a remote and perfect-looking figure in a brief white leotard, and as he speaks I listen intently for I know no one who talks like Erick.

Among other things, he has told us why the Indian bow and arrow works so well, and how he shortened a European visit after hearing the terrifying sound of the Nazi goose step. He has described the character-revealing aspects of ordinary movement, and has instructed us to visit the Museum of Modern Art. This Saturday's topic seems to be radio, for he is saying, "In our society, today, we are inundated by noises; we do not hear any more. We fill the air with more noise, keep the radio going constantly, but we do not listen. We are forgetting how to hear." The class is intrigued but restless. Children of the radio age, we are in sympathy with the pianist who sits patiently waiting for the words to end, for the movement to begin.

A small woman appears at the doorway to the room and pauses for a moment. Quietly, she enters the classroom and sits down on a narrow bench. We glance at one another. It is Martha Graham. Erick goes on with the class. Martha Graham sits on the backless bench as though sitting on a throne. She sits like that, motionless and concentrated, until the end of our lesson. We are fascinated by her presence in the classroom and keep stealing glances at her, while her eyes follow our teacher, Erick Hawkins.

We have heard about Martha's and Erick's recent marriage, and for the rest of that Saturday morning we pay more attention to their romance than to our own work. We follow every one of their glances with unabashed curiosity, and when the class is finally over, we rush into the dressing room. Once inside the door, someone starts, "Did you see the way she was looking at him?" "How old do you think she is?" "How old is he?" "Did they really get married?" Our giggles are our only real answers; that is all we know.

The shadow of the Louisville Symphony Orchestra is seen silhouetted on a translucent screen. Alone on stage in front of the screen is Martha Graham. The orchestra, and Martha Graham, are about to present the

New York premiere of the ballet *Judith*, choreographed by Martha Graham on commission from the orchestra.

Music comes from behind the screen; Graham coils, her body in anguish as she begins to dance the Biblical story of a woman's vengeance. Graham's knee comes up to her chest, her back curves slightly forward, and now her leg, knee leading, juts inward, circles out, in, out again, while her arms swoop through the air like a bird's wings. Through her dance movement, Graham speaks of the turbulent emotions lying deep within Judith's body. We in the audience sit, absorbed, watching Graham search through primitive lusts, while on stage the dance nears its end as she approaches the tent of Judith's enemy, Holofernes. An appreciative audience applauds this searing look at our deepest passions, for we all have some knowledge of hatred, revenge, and righteousness.

It is nine A.M. on December 30, 1950, the morning after the Carnegie Hall performance of *Judith*. Students in the Christmas course held annually at the Martha Graham School of Contemporary Dance wait for the morning's class to begin. Martha Graham is scheduled to teach, but no one really expects her to come to the school this morning. The students are sitting on the floor chatting about last night's performance. "Did you go to the performance last night?" "What did you think of *Judith*?" "That was quite a solo, about twenty-five minutes." "Who do you think will teach this morning?" The room is suddenly silent, and a hush replaces the sound of voices.

Martha Graham walks quietly into the classroom and sits down on a small bench facing the group of student dancers. Amazement generates an electricity that fills the room like the music of a silent orchestra. Martha Graham smiles and quietly murmurs, "Good morning. Bob Cohan will demonstrate today." Classroom discipline is observed: we are all silent. It is as if the event of the night before had not taken place. Martha Graham makes no reference to her solo performance of *Judith*. Instead, she turns to Bob. "Are you ready? Then we will start with the bounces. And a . . . one." The Biblical Judith is back in the Bible, but the mythical Martha is in front of us, teaching. We are witness to and participants in a grand performance.

Connecticut College for Women during the summer dance session in 1954: Martha Graham is facing a gymnasium crowded with students who have come from all over the country to attend the Connecticut College Summer Dance Session. Her voice is emphatic as she scolds the students, "*Pull, pull* on the contraction, don't cave in. And the contraction is *not* a position. It is a movement into something. It is like a pebble, which you

The sculptured look of her famous face. Martha Graham
(Courtesy of the Martha Graham Dance Company)

throw into the water, and then when it hits the water . . . makes rippling circles around it. The contraction moves.''

How many students has Martha Graham taught? She started teaching at Denishawn in 1919, and so 1954 makes thirty-five years of teaching dance to class after class of students. Yet her classes are never boring. If she finds it tedious to be constantly teaching young hopeful dance students to be aware of their bodies, it is her secret. My concentration has slowly shifted from my body to this reverie, and now someone pouncing on my leg forces me back into the present. Hands pull my leg up, way up, and Martha Graham's voice admonishes me, "Light of my life, like this, higher."

It is the 1960's, and the Martha Graham Dance Company is touring in Europe and Israel. The evening's program I see in Israel, *Secular Games*, *Seraphic Dialogue*, and *Phaedra*, is a stimulating and typical encounter with Martha Graham's mythical dance-theatre works. The dancers in the Martha Graham Dance Company (many of them have been with the Company for years) are in top form, dancing with intelligence, strength, and beauty.

As a dancer, Martha Graham, now as always, is a dramatic figure on stage. But in *Phaedra*, she falters while balancing; the theatrical illusion of creating a character on stage through the medium of dance is lost. Instead, I see a great dancer using her dramatic talent to cover her inability to sustain the physicality of the dancer's language. At sixty-seven, Martha Graham's artistic and choreographic visions are stronger and more pliable than her body. She is still remarkably agile, but there is a noticeable difference between her dancing and that of the rest of the Martha Graham Dance Company. Watching her heroic effort is upsetting, and I don't know whether to admire her courage or to cry at the futile hope of reversing time.

It is October 1970. The place is the stage of the Brooklyn Academy of Music. Mayor John Lindsay is presenting Martha Graham with New York City's highest award for cultural achievement, the Handel Medallion. Accepting the award, Martha Graham denies the morning's newspaper story reporting her intention to retire from the stage.

She then goes on in a relaxed manner to share her thoughts with a surprised audience. Among the disparate things running through her mind at the moment are her views on contemporary fashion, musings about the beauty of sea shells, and reminiscences of her youth. She transforms a perfunctory acceptance speech into a choreographed voyage through her mind. When she finishes, an enchanted audience gives her a standing ovation.

By 1970, the year the Handel Medallion was awarded to Martha

Graham, she had stopped dancing on stage, she had stopped doing any new choreography, and she had been away from her school. Two years later, in 1972, I'm surprised by an unexpected invitation to attend some performances at the Martha Graham Center. The twenty-one studio performances at the school are to be the Graham Company's spring season. Company dancers Bertram Ross, Helen McGehee, and Mary Hinkson, who are trying to keep the Graham Company alive, are responsible for the season.

The studio performances are a brave, if not quite successful effort. The younger dancers lack the intensity of past Graham Company dancers, and the limited performing space tightens the choreography into a physicality devoid of spirit. Leaving the School with some dance friends, we start to ask each other the question that everyone in New York's dance world is asking: "What is going to happen to the Martha Graham School of Contemporary Dance and to the Company?" Len is on the New York State Council of the Arts, and he tells us that there is a plan to film all the works that have been revived, but that money is a problem.

We reply as a chorus, "The Company should certainly get funds. Well," we go on, "do you think the Company will continue to go on without her?"

"That," says Len, "is one of the problems with funding."

I get an absurd idea, "Perhaps *Appalachian Spring* should go into American Ballet Theatre's repertoire, like Limon's *Moor's Pavane?*"

Linda says, "The repertoire should be saved, but she would never allow it to go into a ballet company."

Someone else adds, "Will they continue to teach Graham technique at the School?"

Lots of questions; everyone has questions, but only Martha Graham has the answers.

So when I saw an item in the *New York Times* one morning in 1973 saying that Martha Graham had scheduled a short Broadway season in May, I knew that she had answered all those questions by again becoming actively involved with her dance company. She would not be dancing, but she would be choreographing two new works, rehearsing the Company. Age had not gone away, but Martha Graham was back in business. It was good news.

At that time, I was doing the radio program. I called the office at the Graham School, and asked what the chances were for an interview.

The office referred me to a press agent, Tom Kerrigan, whom I happened to know from the Brooklyn Academy of Music. He arranged a short interview for me with Martha Graham at her apartment.

The day for the interview arrived—a sunny April day. Suddenly I felt nervous. I checked my tape recorder over and over to make sure it was working properly. I went over the questions again and again, and I arrived at Martha Graham's apartment house about twenty minutes early. I started to walk around the block. My thoughts were in a jumble, alternating between my personal feelings about the interview, and my rehearsal of a series of planned questions. I had not been at the Graham School for many years, and I could not be casual about the next hour. I had studied with Martha Graham, she had had a strong influence on my life, and I still thought she was the most extraordinary woman I had ever met. I kept walking and, fortunately, passed a flower store with a window full of vivid spring flowers. I bought a bouquet and immediately felt better. Now, I would not arrive with only a tape recorder to record her words, I would come to her door with a gift, a small, symbolic gesture of thanks.

The door of the apartment opens. Ron Protas, Miss Graham's manager, shows me in and tells me that Martha Graham will be out in a moment. A small woman comes quietly into the living room. She is wearing a long gown, her bearing is proud, and her hair is pulled severely back in a chignon, exaggerating the sculptured look of her famous face. I hear her distinctive, contralto voice, "Good morning. Thank you. The flowers are beautiful."

Tom introduces me, we sit down, and coffee is brought out. "Miss Graham, when I was young, I studied at your school."

"Oh," said Miss Graham, "everyone tells me they have studied with me at one time or another. Sometimes I think I have taught half the world. There is a television cowboy star who claims that he falls off a horse so well because he studied dance with me. And Gregory Peck has been very helpful to the Company."

We drink coffee and nibble coffeecakes. I admire a red-laquered Chinese bed standing near the window in a corner of the living room. It would be nice to sit and talk without a time limit, but there is a heavy work schedule to get the Company ready for the upcoming performances.

As we start the interview, I look at Martha Graham's extraordinary face and find it as strikingly expressive as the first time I saw her, in the old studio when I took my first of those Saturday afternoon classes. I try to keep to my prearranged questions, but her answers fascinate me and I find I am easily distracted from my plan. Her dynamic and inspiring way of perceiving life has not changed over the years. The originality of her insights is still compelling, and, of course, remains a unique source of her artistic power.

e.r. *Miss Graham, how did you decide to become a dancer?*
m.g. I think I did not decide, I think it just happened. I had no dance lessons as a child; I wasn't subjected to dance. I lived in Pittsburgh. My mother's people came from a strong Puritan background where such levity was not encouraged, and I knew nothing about the theatre. Then one day we went to Atlantic City for a holiday; I think I was about four, judging by the time my sisters were born, and I saw a Punch and Judy show. Well, that was the complete revelation of the

world. It meant there was another world; it meant there was a window onto something. I can remember sitting in a Victorian drawing room in the hotel, on one of those green—they're always green—velvet poufs with my legs stuck straight out in front of me; it's almost a photographic memory—and seeing the Punch and Judy. And then there was a wait; I didn't do any dancing. We went to California, and there I took my little dancing slippers in my bag and went to ballroom dancing every Saturday. I was bored with that. Then I saw a photograph of Ruth St. Denis dancing in Los Angeles and made my father's life a little complicated until he decided to take me there. So we saw Ruth St. Denis and from that moment out, I was finished. I was going to find that world. And that's how I became a dancer.

e.r. *Did you know at the time about the involvement and the commitment that it would take from your life?*

m.g. No. I knew nothing about it. I knew nothing about the theatre, in the sense that I had never met a dancer. I was still in high school, just beginning, and I would go in summers to a summer school at Denishawn. We lived in Santa Barbara at that time, and it was a darling little Spanish town, but there was nothing there. As soon as I graduated from school, I went to Denishawn. And very shortly found myself in the company as an exotic walk-on, until I learned enough technique to be able to dance.

e.r. *Why did they put you on as an exotic kind of walk-on? What does that mean?*

m.g. It means that I was evidently born with this ability to use fabric, material, veils, anything, and I had no fear. I felt that I belonged there, and I could walk across the stage, and at least I wasn't an obtrusion. I remember one time with Ruth St. Denis, we were on tour, and I was supposed to be her little handmaiden in the East Indian scene. There were three little girls and they were dancing, not very well, and a young, callow boy lying on a couch as a prince, and Miss Ruth said, "Now Martha, you'll just have to go on in that East Indian scene tonight. It lets down in the middle and I cannot get the audience back again." And I said, "Miss Ruth, there are three girls out there dancing as it is, and Robert Gorham." "That means absolutely nothing," she said, and I said, "What shall I do?" "Anything," Miss Ruth said. "Just go and get the chartreuse and cherry colored sari from Pearl, and just go on." And so I did, moving around in choreographed so-called bits and pieces until "the favorite" arrived. Well, that was all right, but one day, when I was making a salaam to greet the favorite in *Black and Gold Sari*—and Miss Ruth was marvelous in that—well, the dresser had got Miss Ruth into the wrong costume and she was in full Japanese regalia. There she was, standing in the wings, wig, pins, kimono, obi, tapi; she looked at me as though she were thunderstruck and said in gestures, "Go on, go on, keep it going." So I had to improvise on the stage while she changed her costume. Now I knew *Black and Gold Sari* inside-out as far as the dance was concerned, but I didn't dare do it. So I don't know what I did. By that time I was in such a dither. And Louis Horst, who was the musical director at that time, was standing in the pit "Stand by to cut, stand by to cut, zzz." Finally, Miss Ruth came on. And that was my theatre training. My craft training was a different matter.

e.r. *By craft, you mean technique?*

m.g. Technique, yes. That was rigid.

e.r. *With Ruth St. Denis at Denishawn?*

m.g. Yes.

e.r. *At that time, did it cover all areas of dance? From what I've read of Denishawn, there was some Spanish, some Indian.*

m.g. Yes, and we had a ballet base.

e.r. *And a ballet base?*

m.g. Yes. The dance technique covered the areas that Miss St. Denis believed in very much and was deeply interested in. I think she was not deeply interested in ballet as such, although she had danced that kind of dance when she was with Belasco. But we had classes in ballet, and so we were taught in the classical way; not, however on pointe.

e.r. *Just a ballet barre. Do you think that's a good approach to the training of a dancer, the interchangeability of several disciplines?*

m.g. Yes, I do. I think it's very important. And of course, in dance, there are no other terms except action terms, which you do find in ballet. And that's very helpful. Modern dance hasn't yet got to that point. There are certain action terms like contraction, release, and so on, but with ballet there are many. Whether it's *echappé* or *assemblé*, or any of them, they are action terms, they are exactly what you do: you bring your legs together, *rrrr*. I think it's very beneficial, particularly today. We have no basic, exclusive classicism as such. We are in the midst of forming things, again.

e.r. *One discipline seems to be influencing the other.*

m.g. Yes. I know the poem that I'm using in the new work, *Mendicants of Evening*, is from St. John Perse, and there's one wonderful phrase in his poem. One wonderful line in which he speaks about, "It's not death, it's not ashes, it's embers," but, "divine turbulence be ours, to the last eddy, we settle, not for the least, not for the worst, but divine turbulence be ours." I missed on that last line; I can't quote it exactly. But that is a stage that in a way we're in now. Only it isn't quite so divine. We hope the result will be divine. Not only in the dance, but in life itself. Because whatever one is, or whatever one dances, one is. In a deep way, yes. It's reflected in theatre, and in all expressions of the arts of man.

e.r. *Yes, very much so. For me, that's part of the whole reason of the existence for any art. Also, that people can extend their own personal knowledge and experience through what someone else has been able to see, to find, or discover.*

m.g. Yes. Dance, when it came in as modern, or what is called modern—it's a dreadful term, but we got saddled with it—there is nothing else—was a catalytic agent. It charged everything, it set fire to certain things. It was a great nuisance to many people who are supreme classicists. I always remember Mrs. Isaacs, who was the editor and founder of *Theatre Arts Monthly*, a great, great, lady, and she said that modern dance was the unspanked baby of the American stage, which it was at that time. I'm not sure we're completely out of that period yet.

e.r. *I remember from years ago, that I always felt that a good class in Graham technique was a very beautiful thing to watch. And one of the things that I liked very much was the involvement of the breath, and the shifting of weight in dynamics. To me, that was something that I fell in love with at the time. I thought it was so exciting. Maybe it exists in all very good dancing, but I don't know of anything else, at least in my experience, that uses that shifting of body weight in the way that you have. That was your discovery, or the use of the body's breathing as a dynamic emotional force.*

m.g. Well, I'm not sure about that. I know we go back to something called phrase, and phrase means, as you know—and this is probably the reason why you are in literature or writing—phrase means length of time. Breath length if you're angry, it's a short breath, it's a short phrase. If you are in a love scene, like Tristan and Isolde, it goes on forever, you're in a l-o-o-ng phrase. And I think it was the dynamics of feeling that the dancer became involved with, and that is only accomplished through breath, because that's what phrase means, breath.

e.r. *As you developed your own works, as a choreographer, did the technique develop with it? Did it all flow because of what movement meant to you? Is that really what happened?*

m.g. Yes, I felt that. As much as I can be articulate about it, there was so much more that we were not using. There was so much to be discovered. There was such a wealth of experience within the memory of man, not even conscious memory, and I wanted to dance what I was. As it says, ''You have so little time to be born to the instant.'' And it is that, that the dancer is. You have to feel with the dancer such churning and such possession by this training and wonderment, so as to feel that you are looking at something for the first time. It's newborn. That instant, it's never been done before. And it is the wonder of that which makes dance such a lodestone, I think. It's like a lovely horse. You see this lovely, lovely thing and he's so charged. Like those horses in Vienna, those trained white stallions, and he loves what he does, he isn't put upon for one moment, he's dying to get on that stage. I know when I was in vaudeville with a cockatoo, an act of cockatoos; I go back. There was one cockatoo, named Ethel, and for some unknown reason, Ethel did not like me. Ethel was seventy-five years old that they knew of, and she had no feathers around her neck so she couldn't go out on the stage. She had a little disease or something, but Ethel would be shut in the dressing room when what they called the act of cockatoos was on. Oh, they had a fire engine and all that kind of thing, you know, vaudeville was an old-fashioned thing. And the minute the music started, Ethel would bounce up and down and scream her head off because she wanted to get on that stage, and she was going to. She would see me coming and she knew I was afraid of her, and I'm not afraid of animals at all, and she'd spread her wings and hiss and put her bill out in front of her, and I just disappeared. Ethel was too much for me. But that thing that you see in an animal, in a beautiful animal, you look for it in the bones of a dancer. The bones of the face, actually the bones are the one thing that really lasts the longest after death or after any change. The bones are very beautiful. I know the masseur that I go to has a spine on his wall. It's real and it's perfect. It's one of the most beautiful things. It's like a great flower, and I can understand how the cult of the Kundalini [yoga] came into being—the cult of the snake—because in Indian [Kundalini] yoga there is the serpent that lies at the base of the spine and lifts himself until the head is spread. Unless you've got the kundalini coming up, I'm sorry there isn't very much. You need *that* to be a dancer. It's that will to move, like watching a baby try and learn to turn over in a crib. The fury it manifests when it gets over once and then can't get over the next time. I saw it happen with a little baby. I was fascinated because that will, that little will to be alive, to get on its little legs, to move, to feel, is so strong.

e.r. *I understand you're now preparing two new works for the company's season.*

m.g. One is called *Mendicants of Evening*. It is a title that comes from the poem of St. John Perse called *Chronique*. He was an ambassador to this country, he's French, or at least he was in the embassy to this country during the Vichy regime. He didn't go back until the war was over. This is the poem that St. John Perse read when he received the Nobel prize for peace or literature, I forget which. There are two firsts in this work, one is that I'm using electronic music for the first

The feeling of a ritual. Martha Graham and members of her company in **Primitive Mysteries** *(Courtesy of the Dance Collection, New York Public Library at Lincoln Center)*

time. The score was not written for me, I heard it, and it was perfect for this piece. It's a fine, delicate web of sound against which you move, and some of it is very beautiful. The other first is that I have never used a painted backdrop before, and this one is painted. It's a very large painting by Mr. Fangor, he's had exhibits here at the Guggenheim, and so on, and this painting that he did for this piece has an opening which you can come through. I've always used sculpture on the stage, because I've used sculpture as people, as creative, moving objects. And in this I'm not. I'm letting the light on the set dominate. Take the visual for one part, and the sound for another part, but there isn't a story line in any sense. It's what I believe that St. John Perse meant in that it is a reiteration of faith. It's an act of faith in the sense that I've used it. I've not used it in the religious way because I only use religion on the stage as theatre, not as a religious cult or any propaganda.

e.r. *As a poetic feeling?*

m.g. Yes. It's a sense of ritual that reoccurs in *Mendicants of Evening*. The other piece is called *Myth of a Voyage*. It is not a voyage, except as it takes place in any man's experience. It's seen through a man's eyes. It is departure from home, from the establishment, whether it is in his mind or it is actual, and his adventures in the world with various ladies. Then his return, under protest I must say, to his original base. It's not a comedy in any sense, but it is a little ironic. The music is by Alan Hovannes, who had done my work before, and the set is by Ming Cho Lee, with whom I've worked before.

e.r. *Will that also be a painted set, or will it be a sculpture?*

m.g. No, sculpture. These are objects that he has made for the stage. They are not sculpture in the sense of Noguchi's. I know what they are, but I don't want to say exactly. I'd like Ming to say it when it comes time. But they are made to establish an atmosphere.

e.r. *Thank you for the interview, and for everything I've ever learned from you.*

m.g. That's very generous of you to say that, and I've enjoyed you very much.

A small woman, elegantly gowned in black and gold, stands dramatically alone on an empty stage. She waits, motionless as a votive figurine, until the thunderous sound of applause that greets her appearance subsides, before smiling and nodding her head in gracious acknowledgement. Then, in her low, melodious voice, Martha Graham begins the lecture that the opening night audience at the Mark Hellinger Theatre expects as a special introduction to the spring 1974 season of the Martha Graham Dance Company.

Sitting regally in a chair at the edge of the stage, Graham starts the evening by scolding the audience as she might chide students in a classroom. "Theatre was a verb before it was a noun. It was an act before it was a building." Everyone is attentive and obviously captivated by her words and by her performance, which bristles with the authority of a superb theatrical instinct.

Martha Graham speaks fluently, without notes and without an instant's hesitation. Her words and thoughts are illumined by a poetic sensibility, and her imaginative, searching mind constantly seeks confrontations with every aspect of life. Obliquely, Graham refers to the cause of the audience's overwhelming reception. "Relinquishing dance was a great sorrow and a great bitterness. When you've geared your life to dance, your body wants to go on, but time has a curious way of saying 'This far and no further'." The statement is made simply, without self-pity. The effect has a tragic dimension. We in the audience listen and share with her, the devastating power and finality of time and age.

The mood lightens, however, as the twenty-six dancers of the Martha Graham Dance Company come on stage, ready to demonstrate the essentials of Graham technique. As the dancers arrange themselves in a pattern on stage, Graham explains the concept behind the need for technique. "Through technique, one acquires the discipline that, in turn, allows total freedom and a sense of well-being. From that awareness comes the intense 'glow' that makes either a 'hot' dancer or a 'cold' dancer, but not an 'in-between' dancer."

The group, accompanied by only one pianist, as if in an actual class, begins the demonstration on the floor with bounces and stretches that develop into a series of Graham contractions. The work is physically taxing, but the results, evolved from Martha Graham's lifetime study and work with the human body, develops strong, articulate dancers. The dancers are beautiful to watch as they move through a series of falls, but I find that my eyes as well as my ears keep turning to the seated figure of Graham who sagaciously comments: "You must keep alive the wonder. You must listen to ancestral footsteps, but you must never look back. You must move ahead believing movement never lies, searching for truth, letting your body speak, knowing technique prepares your body to speak in dance. Driving yourself because there are sources of energy in your body that make you rise so you are free, and that freedom makes you sure of your moves."

In 1973, when Martha Graham first pulled herself back over the edge of ill health to reassert control of her dance company and to choreograph once again, she unwittingly set in motion an extraordinary epilogue to her life's work. At first, support for her appearances and for her company came from the faithful dance audiences. But when Betty Ford's husband, Gerald Ford, succeeded to the Presidency of the United States in 1974, Graham, through Mrs. Ford's attentions, became a nationally known figure.

Mrs. Ford studied at the Martha Graham School of Dance in New York during the late 1930's and early 1940's. Although she later decided against pursuing a career as a professional dancer, she never forgot her days with Martha Graham. "She [Martha Graham] is my very, very favorite person, one of the outstanding women of the world. She was my teacher and she helped shape my life. She gave me the ability to stand up to all the things I've had to go through with more courage than I would ever have had without her."

The press ran to Martha Graham and she responded with candor and grace. "It's always nice to be remembered in that way and it is unique that a woman so much in the news has said that she studied with me. Very few are so gracious. Part of a training of a dancer is to meet a situation with courage and the necessity for complete honesty." Through this unusual set of circumstances, Martha Graham became a familiar name to the public, though people generally remained unaware of the nature of her work. And there was irony in her popularity. The greatest outpouring of recognition and support that she had ever known came late, years after her own dancing had ended. Audiences now, must seek the rich, performing power of Martha Graham's dancing through the shadow of herself that hovers over the dancers who inherit the famous roles.

Dance, at any time, at any level, is expensive. Sold-out houses help, but costs, especially if a live orchestra is used, cannot be covered by audience attendance alone. Some form of subsidy is necessary, and traditionally this role has been played by governments and wealthy patrons. Now, with Mrs. Ford as honorary chairman, the fashion designer Halston offering jewel encrusted costumes, and Rudolf Nureyev, the ballet superstar, as a guest performer, the first gala for the Martha Graham Dance Company since 1926 took place in June 1975. Martha Graham choreographed *Lucifer* for Nureyev, who had only recently become a private pupil, though he had admired her work since 1967 when he saw her company perform in London. In a sense, Nureyev's Russian, classical ballet training places him in another world. Theirs was an unexpected association, and when asked about it Graham remarked: "He is a romantic Tartar and he insisted. He has an endless capacity for work. It takes courage to break the pattern the audience has made for you. I told him we may fail. If we do, we don't want to make it a little failure, we will make a scandal." With their diligence in reporting, the press corps made a good audience, and with complete seriousness Graham told them . . . "When Lucifer fell, he became half-god, half-man, and subject to the same fate and the same tribulations as all of us." The gala itself was a huge success and enough money came in to offset debts of the Martha Graham Dance Company.

As 1975 ended and 1976 began, the Martha Graham Dance Company celebrated its fiftieth anniversary season with three special gala evenings during a return engagement at the Mark Hellinger Theatre. Since Halston had become a friend, associate, and sponsor of Martha Graham, she had become as much of a social personality as a dance legend. Though rumor made the galas the social event of the season, Graham herself was busy supervising the revival of the 1935 solo, *Frontier*, and choreographing a new work, *The Scarlet Letter*, for Nureyev, who continued as a guest with the company.

At the gala I attended, Aaron Copeland conducted his own score for the lyrical 1944 ballet *Appalachian Spring*. Nureyev danced the role of the preacher, but his interpretation of the role was heavier than the mocking lightness with which Graham saw the character. Graham introduced the evening's program in much the same way as she had at the April 1974 opening night. Then it was part of her new role, exchanging the drama of dancing for the drama of the spoken word. Now, her introductory remarks became the magic draw for which people paid the benefit prices. She cajoled and lectured with a disarming impertinence. "I'm a thief. Don't ever expect to show me a movement that I might not use. I only pride myself that I choose the best." And when she spoke, as she always does, of the act of dancing, she transmitted the white heat of artistic ardor: "The dancer stirs up the gift of God which is within. Beneath the anguish of technique lies a hunger for experience." The audience was hushed, surprised, and delighted. It was being led toward the path of artistic insight by the startling, incandescent woman who sat serenely on the stage, adding to her own legend with every passing instant.

During the last few years, Martha Graham has returned to her craft, creating dance works to add to her repertoire of over 150 ballets. The style of her current choreography is essentially lyrical, though the actual movements tend to have a static quality. The themes revolve around Graham's never ending fascination with the problems and joys flowing from human love. Most of the work of this decade—*O Thou Desire Who Art About to Sing, The Plain of Prayer, Adoration, Shadow, Flute of Pan, The Scarlet Letter, The Owl and the Pussycat, Ecuatorial*—is developed simply, without the mythical plots, heroines, and dramatic narrative episodes of her earlier psychological and mythical artistic periods. But Graham is still intent on searching deep into the human passions, and she explores the power of love's memories, the anguish of betrayal, the effects of irony, the injustice of disgrace. The unique, ever-present sense of poetic imagery in her dances gives her choreography, of whatever period, the undeniable, brilliant stamp of a Graham work, as does the presence of striking sets and props designed by contemporary artists for each ballet.

Along with the premieres of new Graham works, special galas, and introductory lectures, the newly annual New York dance seasons of the Martha Graham Dance Company also include revivals from the 1930's (*Frontier, Primitive Mysteries*) and the 1940's (*Death and Entrances, Dark Meadow, Errand Into the Maze*) as well as later works like *Seraphic Dialogue* and *Phaedra*. I find this unusual retrospective of the Graham repertoire an exciting opportunity to experience the full scope of her choreographic wanderings. Previously, the programs were essentially of the period and style with which Graham was currently working, and it is only in recent years that there has been any attempt to recreate the "historical" ballets of earlier decades.

Originally premiered on February 2, 1931, *Primitive Mysteries* is one of the keystone works performed by the first Martha Graham Dance Company. The work was revived during the late 1960's at the Connecticut College Summer Dance Session, but I missed it there, and so I was full of anticipation when I at last had the opportunity to see the legendary work. The Lunt-Fontanne Theatre was filled to capacity on that 1977 spring evening, and in the audience I spotted members of the early company who had helped bring about this revival, as well as younger dancers who had come for a first-hand look at their modern dance roots.

The program notes described *Primitive Mysteries* as "literally a celebration of the coming of age of a girl. It has its beginnings in the adoration of the Virgin as experienced in the Southwestern, Spanish-American culture." In addition to choreographing the work, Martha Graham designed the costumes. Louis Horst, Graham's associate and mentor for many years, composed the original piano score. The ballet opens as a procession of twelve girls, dressed in black, . . . simply and dramatically cross the stage. They hold their arms tightly to their sides; they keep their bodies still and walk proudly, marking out a ritual path across the empty space. Three times they enter and exit, using a deliberate, weighty walk. With each entry, they enact a segment of their private ritual. Power builds gradually, inevitably, until the seated, central figure in white (originally danced by Martha Graham) is encircled by the pounding, leaping group of girls. There is a feeling of foreboding in the group's gestures. It is resolved by the last section as, triumphantly, the group accepts the figure in white. Then, arms tightly held, bodies still, the procession leaves, marking out a path with their strong, silent feet.

Though the program notes cast the ritual of *Primitive Mysteries* in a vague religious light, the ceremony within the ballet can also be symbolically interpreted as Martha Graham's dedication of herself to the art of dance. Since her Denishawn days in the 1920's, Graham's life has been a commitment of love, struggle, and courage. The art world has always been supportive of her work, recognizing its validity and its contribution to the arts of the United States. Now, with the popularization of the Martha Graham legend, she has become known to the general public, and much is known about her personally. Nevertheless, there is still some confusion about her work. Audiences limited to experiencing the classical ballet are somewhat at a loss when they first encounter the dance theatre of Martha Graham. Martha Graham has an indomitable spirit, however, and at eighty-five she continues to travel with her company in Europe and across the United States, instructing and inspiring those who listen to her as she reflects on the essence of dance and of life.

A Lesson with Erick Hawkins

They've got to see you be on the knife's edge.

I SIT ON A LOW, WOODEN BENCH in a corner of the studio and watch the strong light of the late afternoon sun sweep through the room's empty space. It's a midsummer day in 1978, and like the dancers, who one by one saunter in to the empty studio, I'm waiting for Erick Hawkins to teach the advanced dance class, scheduled for four-thirty this afternoon. But unlike the dancers, who are busy warming up their muscles for the upcoming class, I'm a quiet observer, busy with the echo of old, hopeful emotions tearing through my mind and body.

I gaze at the dancers who lie on the floor in the afternoon heat, stretching their backs, and I recall the innumerable times that I did the same while preparing for a class with Erick. Though I see technical differences between the exercises I had done and those being done now by the nine women and three men who make up this class at the Erick Hawkins School of Dance, their motions are so familiar that the intervening decades, since my teen-age years as Erick's student in classes at the Martha Graham School of Contemporary Dance, appear to be nothing more than a long night's sleep. In fact, my memories can easily be superimposed over today's experience. Even the atmosphere is similar to the one I remember. The sparse, clean dressing rooms, the airy studio with a grand piano in one corner, a low wooden bench against the wall, and above all, the serious, intense expressions of the dancers as they prepare themselves for the class—all are still there.

The dancers have been stretching for ten minutes or so when Erick enters the studio. He immediately walks across the room to the huge loft windows and closes all but the small corner one. "If it gets too hot, we can put that on," he says, pointing to a small electric fan sitting on the window sill. Striding over to the center of the room, he positions himself with his back to the mirror and faces the group of attentive students.

Erick is well past middle age, and except for the color of his hair, now an odd, sandy white, he appears very much the same as when I first saw him thirty years ago. His proud, erect body, clad like all his students in a one-piece tank-style leotard, is still trim, while his bare legs offer a prideful challenge to advancing age. By chance, Erick underscores his preference for habitually working without tights when, later on in the class, he stops the work to comment on the group's experience of the previous day while performing for a visiting group of Chinese dancers. "They're so puritanical,'' he says in amazement, ''that we were asked to wear tights. I don't know what there is about bare legs that's so bad, but in their country, it seems that sex is controlled to some extent by the state. But I did tell them something very wonderful which they liked, that we're beautiful animals with beautiful souls.''

The class begins in earnest. ''Let your arms breathe,'' he instructs as the class follows him. ''If you do it with momentum, you'll get the swing all in one piece.''

After the *pliés* come the brushes. Standing on one leg, the students stretch out the other directly in front, foot pointed, toe on the floor, then draw it back to center balance. The class knows the exercise, but Erick is after a quality in the movement and admonishes, ''The problem's to get the right sensibility, to move, but to keep sensing the softness. I don't mean a namby-pamby softness.''

Following Erick, the dancers continue on through the routine of specially designed exercises that build into a dance technique. As Erick's mind is now on something else, he stops the class to ask if anyone knows the painting of . . . No one is acquainted with the work, but the question has essentially been a rhetorical one, and so Erick instructs, ''Just as well no one knows his work, because it's a bunch of hogwash. To put colors together doesn't necessarily create an art object. It's too infantile. There's got to be something of interest in how it is done. Get the point? To make art, you get a motif. With movement, you must have interest in how it's done.''

It's no wonder I have this uncanny feeling of reliving my teenage years. Erick is just the same as I remember him. Perhaps his musings during a lesson of years ago would have centered on a different topic, but the pattern of instruction would have been identical. For Erick's thoughts about life are as integral a part of his classes as are the physical exercises. In fact, Erick's musings so many years ago acted as my introduction to a supersensitive awareness. Like many of his students, I've often been surprised by his words and thankful for the ideal which he has consistently projected as a guide, not only for dance, but for living. For Erick, his years of aesthetic instruction to the countless students in his workshops and classes seem to be as important to his role as an artist as is the audience who comes to see his finished work.

This class listens patiently, their very presence showing a willingness to hear his ideas. And when, as now, he seemingly departs entirely from classwork to talk of something unrelated, they are attentive. ''I finished reading my Lindbergh book last night. He had a long stretch without sleep and speaks of the phantoms that appeared in his exhaustion. The agony of not having sleep.'' Erick's tone is confidential, and connecting

A strong, charismatic Erick Hawkins . . . (Photo: Michael Avedon)

Lindbergh's experience to that of the dancers, he adds, "You have to pour it all out, even if you don't feel like it."

There isn't any musical accompaniment for today's class, so in addition to comments, corrections, and philosophizing, Erick keeps a rhythm going by counting. "Four, five, one, reach," he half-sings, half-barks while the class develops a sidestep turn with torso and arms lifting. A series of circular leg patterns done in a parallel position follows, but the movement is stopped by Erick. "The phrase has to have a dynamic journey. Take some kind of movement and make it interesting. That's what makes a dancer. There's going to be competition; it's not an old-age home. You can't say it's all brotherly love. If you're after a booking, you're going to compete with another company. To get it, you have to interest people. With the dancers, it's the same; to get the roles, you have to interest people."

The class moves slowly but serenely and I particularly admire the unusually liquid feeling of movement projected by the students in all their work. It is the same style of moving which I've previously enjoyed watching during performances of the Erick Hawkins Dance Company. Physically, it evolves out of an awareness of the joints, and theoretically, it is an important concept in the technique that Erick has developed over the last few decades. Even in this advanced class, he stops the work to stress this aspect. "I've never seen anyone work the way I have, up and down, to get the joints of the legs going smoothly. One reason that I don't like ballet is because in the *relevé*, the weight of the body is just pushed up straight rather than out of the oneness."

The dancers nod and bend and flex their joints to keep their muscles warm during this short inactive spell while Erick is speaking. The hour-and-a-half class has nearly ended when something else occurs to Erick as the students move across the floor in a stylized walk, and he asks, "Why did I use paper in my white cloud dance?" There is some stretching of feet and shifting of weight in the dancers' postures as they consider the question, but only one or two of the dancers offer tentative answers. Ultimately the answer has to be Erick's, as they know, and he states, "Hopefully to get interesting movement. If it ain't there, there's nothing for the audience to see."

We had taped a conversation some time before, so when the class finishes, I thank Erick for letting me observe and leave. When I reach the street, I stop and shake my head in disbelief. Erick's present studio is only a few doors away from the school where I first saw him so many years ago. After the last hour-and-a-half, I feel as though everything, and yet nothing, has changed. To me there's been something unreal about the afternoon's experience. It's as though time has stopped in order to allow the past to represent itself as the present. But time has passed, not stopped; it's my feelings that remain unchanged. For whatever changes or transformations have occurred in the years since I was thirteen, Erick has remained a man imbued with the spirit of aesthetic enlightenment, and I am still in awe of his tireless, proselytizing zeal.

e.r. *The titles of your new works,* Angels of the Inmost Heaven, Dawn Dazzled Door, *and* Classic Kite Tails, *are very poetic. They seem to describe a mood or essence rather than a literal experience. Is your approach to the dance, and to these pieces, based on a poetic vision? What did you have in mind when you chose those titles? I haven't seen the dances yet.*

e.h. We use the word "poetic," with several aspects, several meanings. I studied Greek when I was in college, and I know that the word poetry comes from *poesis*, which means "a making." So a poet is a maker in that sense, which is a good way of saying that an artist is someone who, compared to a person who's not an artist, is making something with the materials that we roughly call art. Generally, though, we use "poetic" to mean something more highly formed. We say it's poetic if it has some very special highlighting, some essential aspect brought out.

e.r. *Do you think the idea of something being poetic implies that it is outside of daily living?*

e.h. What I'm very sad about is that in our present day society, it's easy to adapt to the values of machine-made comfort. We've lost our basic relation to nature. When a people, whether primitive or sophisticated, feel close to nature, they're apt to look at it with wonder and express themselves poetically. Poetry is a way of speaking of one of the very essences of human existence. What kind of art is there that's worth a damn that isn't poetic? I'm flattered when you say that those titles are poetic, because that's what I aim at. What I hope is that the titles of a dance should verbally convey some of the poetic essence of what the movement is going to show. A movement that's not poetic is dull.

e.r. *You do connect with essence. In an article that I've read about your work, you emphasized that you seek to express nature in your work; that a connection to nature is your motivation.*

e.h. The whole dance field uses human movement in a way no other group does, and I feel that they as well as all people in our society, have to look at our human body as part of nature. We have the same seven vertebrae in our neck that a giraffe has. We have the same sevenness that a dolphin has. I looked at a skeleton of a dolphin in the museum, and its seven vertebrae could be put like seven quarters between your two fingers, but that mystery and that same sevenness is there.

One of the sad things I see as I watch people walk around the street is a kind of separation from some very normal principles of movement. I guess, from the very beginning of my work, I sensed that if we were going to have a new American dance that would be of any worth, we had to learn the laws of movement according to the normal principles of natural movement. We couldn't base an art of dance on anything that violated the body. What I'm talking about is the necessity of thinking how, in dance, and then in daily life, each of us can learn to obey the laws of natural movement so that we move with grace and efficiency.

I've always felt that the dance that came from Europe in the past—historically, no blame—simply had not looked at the laws of movement. For example, I may be an iconoclast, but I think the toe shoe is just as silly as the way, not too long ago, Chinese aristocrats bound women's feet. Last year, I talked to a young Chinese of a well-to-do family, and he remembers his father, who was rather liberated, having to argue with the daughter and the mother about binding the daughter's feet. The father said, "No," but the daughter wanted to do it. To me, that's just as bad as a little girl who, through imitating an idea, wants to get up there in that brutal toe shoe. If you've ever looked at the feet of anyone who has danced in toe shoes! The girl who broke my nose in my early ballet training had feet that were a mess. My own feeling is that our body should not be violated by an idea like that. And, of course, I take my greatest inspiration from Isadora Duncan, who really had the first vision of natural dance in two thousand years in the Western world.

Today, in America, we have the chance to approach some beautiful norm of what the human being can be. That concept of movement affects the way I teach my class. Instead of treating the back as something as rigid as a poker, so that you lift up the legs over some sort of a semaphore, I'm saying that when you move one part of the leg, something else in the spine will always move at that same moment. That physical feeling of the relation of bodily parts, a kind of totality, is a very important aspect of what I think will be a new dance. Not to let something outside the mind guide the movement in dance, not some image of a kind of geometry, a diagram, but, instead, to let something that comes a bit more from shifts of weight form the movement. And so on the very first level, you might say, obeying nature could be something that on the technical side is needed in our dance art.

But there is also another aspect, what you communicate in the art; what you talk about, what these poetic titles say. It happens that we've been in the age of Freudianism, and curiously, a degree of spiritual disintegration has followed. I'm alluding to the theatre of the absurd, anarchy, nihilism, dadaism, that sort of thing. Ideas that are an odd probing around down in the messy part of human beings, when everyone knows if there's a mess, the goal is to get out of it. You don't stay and wallow around in the mess. I, personally, start to think about the starting point, the metaphor of a dance, by using nature.

e.r. *By metaphor of a dance, do you refer to the overall symbolic meaning of a dance piece?*

e.h. Yes. Curiously enough, the way to make beautiful movement, just for the sheer beauty of it, but also to have it relate to something a little larger than just pure movement, is to use that very beautiful device of art, the metaphor. I've created many dances that are simply pure movement, but with the use of metaphor, one is not only doing the beautiful movement, but also relating to many other things in the world. One dance that we performed in 1960 was called *Eight Clear Places*, not eight murky places, not eight neurotic places, but eight clear places. And if you speak about eight clear places in nature, maybe you can arrive at eight clear places in the human soul, too. Consider, for example, the first main solo in the piece, a simple pine tree. It's a solo for myself, but how does a human man dance a pine tree? To be effective, there has to be a metaphorical symbolism in the whole pattern of movements. That, I think, ties in somewhat with your first question about the sense of poetry in the titles, because one of the most beautiful ways dance can be poetic is through metaphor.

People have always imitated animals in their dancing. Most primitive societies have done it. For example, I've seen it in the dance of the Hopis out in Arizona, where I was born—anyhow pretty close, in Colorado. Some of the most important influences on my art have come from the very beautiful Appolonian art of the Hopi dances and masks. They have "kachina" masks of the sun and many other kinds of objects. Part of what I'd like to get across to Americans is that poetry is always a little wondrous and a little strange. It's never literal or journalistic, it's not naive or realistic like that stupid pop art where, in the most childish way, you take any object from the world around us and just translate it into art. That's a limited idea that'll go out of fashion very quickly, whereas the truly poetic is such an enriching experience, that if I read Homer today, I'm still thrilled by it. Or if I delve into the meditations of a Chinese sage, like Hantze, who lived in 400 B.C., I'm excited because it's still important to our human experience. By the chance of your asking me about the titles of my new dances, I've been going on about this, although poetry does reflect the loveliest attitude that I could speak of. My own working in the dance is influenced by the idea of a poetry that is always loving. I've a strong feeling that the artist should never put on the stage anything that doesn't help the person watching it to be a more beautiful, complete, and mature human being. So, as you can imagine, I disagree with a great deal of art that's offered today.

e.r. *I can see that. Also, just now, you answered a question that I was going to ask you, and that is: what do you want the audience to experience.*

e.h. You remember what Socrates said—it was inscribed over the Temple of the Apollo at Delphi—"Know thyself." We must seek self-knowledge along with an awareness of the spiritual wisdom to be found in every part of the world, including the Hopis or the Navajos. Each of us must become conscious of our own totality and not stay in a little pocket of illusions. We must feel at one with all other peoples in the world and with nature, and not feel as though each of us is a little egotistical center struggling against everyone else. Every religion has said that, and I do think art has to be religious. The first book on dancing that I ever read was *The Art of Dance*, and it was published by the old *Theatre Arts*. It was a marvelous magazine. We've nothing like it today, nothing as serious. The book had a series of essays by Isadora [Duncan], and some about her. In it, she said, "Unless dance is religious, it is mere merchandise." I still feel it to this day. I don't know of any other way except to think of the art of dance as being religious in the sense that it would be a way that the artist is, for the moment, the reflector of consciousness for the people who are not artists at that moment. The next moment, then that artist is going to be in the audience for the painters, or I'm an audience for the poets, and he, the active artist, has to be a priest for me and bracket his experience in some way. It means that you don't pander. You don't sell toothpaste by showing female flesh; there's some other way. But speaking about flesh, in the last performances that I did, I did a dance called *Of Love*, in which the dancers are as bare as works for the idea, and it is meant to be erotic, but not cheesy, and not titillating. That dance is really meant to show how beautiful, how tender, and deeply one, is the relationship between men and women. We have some wonderful pictures of that dance taken by Herb Migdoll.

One of the new dances, *Angels of the Inmost Heaven*, comes from a quote by Swedenborg. Let me see if I can remember it, he said, "In heaven, some of the angels are clothed with fire, and the garments of others glow with light, but the angels of the inmost heaven are not clothed." And I use that as a way of saying something I think very important philosophically. If we human beings ever think our body is dirty and unworthy, we're really torn apart, because we are in our body. So, I guess what I feel, and that's why I think the dance is important, is that it can bring, not only the dancers, but the audience as well, up to a high consciousness of really how beautiful the human

"A comic idea, but without any cruelty." Erick Hawkins with members of his company in **Parson Weems and the Cherry Tree.** *(Photo: Lois Greenfield)*

body can be. If we're going to live our life fully, then it's incumbent for us to nurture it and cultivate it. One can't abuse the body by eating too much or not exercising and so forth. One of the first places of beauty in the world is the human body. Just a couple of days ago, a friend of mine called me and gave me these two statements from [William] Blake: "Man has no body distinct from his soul." Maybe this one is even more pertinent to dance: "That called body is a portion of soul discerned by the five senses." What it means is that there is no split. I think there's not a human being alive, boy or girl, who's grown up, I mean, in our society, and not been troubled by puberty. That's us, we're part of nature. Sometimes people say, "Well, Erick, why don't you go all the way and completely uncover the body?" That's kind of dumb because it is art; this isn't naturalism, and so we do have the briefest of costumes. I wouldn't accept them if I didn't think they were very beautiful. Our costumes do cover us up in such a way so that what you're really seeing is generic man and woman. I think that dancers are really lucky people to be in a profession that keeps their bodies in trim.

e.r. *I know that you feel strongly about using music that is specifically composed for the dance you are choreographing. You don't like to set a dance to music already known.*

e.h. It's a very important aspect. When I first started to dance, I had seen Harold Kreutzburg dance in a beautiful collaboration of dance, music, and visual design. I've hung on to that image, especially of making every dance visually unique. I've been fortunate in having the collaboration of a sculptor, Ralph Dorazio, who is absolutely unique. There is no one else in this country who is willing to make designs in such minute collaboration with the choreographer, and make them so beautifully. Ralph understands something very important that I learned when I first got Isamu [Noguchi] to do many of the designs for Martha Graham. I got the commission for those works, and part of it included Isamu's doing the designs for *Herodiade* and *Appalachian Spring*. At the same time, he did two magnificent sets for me; one for a dance called *John Brown* and another for a dance called *Stephen Acrobat*. The point is, that I saw Isamu bring a very important principle into Western theatre, absolutely revolutionary, and that is, that the backside of anything on stage has to be as beautiful as the frontside. When you look at some of the masks in my work, like the masks from *Eight Clear Places*, they are as beautiful in the back as in the front. For *Dawn Dazzled Door*, the string orchestra sits on the back of the stage and Ralph has made a sculpture that stands on three bamboo legs and goes up to about 16 feet high. It is set on the diagonal, stage left, and then, he's made another sculpture that stands on a tripod. That one is vaguely in the image of a door, but it doesn't look like a door. It's a surface that you can speak of as the door. The other sculpture is almost like the sun, but you understand, that's why it's poetic, it's not literal representation, it's not naive realism. Anyhow, I felt from the first that we had to have a beautiful new visual design for the theatre and get away from realism.

Likewise, I knew that if we were going to have a new American dance, we needed a new American music. So I've held to a very exact platform from the first dance I ever composed. I've never composed a dance to existing music or worked with the music of any composer whom I didn't know or commission, except once. I used a cello sonata of the Hungarian composer, Kodály. It was just the right area for a solo that I did. It was really the first of my naked dances, so to speak. It was even called *Naked Leopard*, but I've always thought that you couldn't have a contemporary dance statement while your ears were hearing old sounds that came out of another period. They had another spirit, another vitality, they were of another moment. My way is risky, because maybe it's not a classic, maybe no one knows whether the music is any good when they hear it for the first time. Maybe they're challenged just to see what's happening to them, they have no kudos, no aura that it's Bach or Beethoven. Do you see, it's much riskier.

One of the first things that some of the early American modern dance artists did was to plan the dance first, and then have the music written. They knew that the general historical way in the West was for the dance to follow the music, but with their new, original vitality, they said, if you're going to have this dance, have it do what it has within it to do. Maybe, for instance, the dance has to break some of its bonds with the music and have the music come after. Now the great problem is, how are you going to get an equally good composer who isn't just a mickey-mouser to write the music? I consider myself, literally, the most fortunate choreographer in American history to have a great composer, like Lucia Dlugoszevski, willing to go into a collaboration with me, but not to go into an egotistical assertion of writing her score. Lucia loved what I did, and has been willing to work on the base of my whole structure, not just the rhythmic structure, but the whole emotional structure, the whole dynamic structure, and create a work that, to the best of her ability, is quite the equal of my structure.

Every once in a while, someone says, "Oh, we don't like the dance at all, but we loved this new music." That's fine. Sometimes, people say when I'm performing, "Oh, goodness, the music was so interesting, Mr. Hawkins, I was listening to the music being played, and I hardly watched the dance." I say, "That's fine, just come see it all again." You know, I've had critics tell me, "Why, we don't hear the music.'' I had an important critic say to me, ''I almost never hear the music.'' Well, dammit, if your art is good, you've got to be conscious of all of the elements, otherwise don't have them there.

The risk of making this new art was to try the new composers and develop them. I think the dancers will do the contemporary music people a great service to keep them physical, so they stop this bookish, structural, stopwatch, paper music that no one wants to hear because it's so unphysical. Maybe by working with the dance, composers can really be revitalized, because our body rhythms are the very essence of our existence. When this heart stops beating in its beautiful regularity, we're done, and no machine is going to take our place. One of the things that I feel very strongly about is never dancing to a tape or a record. I never have and I never will. Not even on tour, nohow, for me that would be death. That's as though I would say, can the dancers make some kind of a robot, and let them do it and call it dancing. I just feel that the whole point is to keep this vitality from our very body existence, our man-to-man-ness, our person-to-person experience. The people have got to come to the theatre and see you sweat. They've got to come and see you be ready to fall on your ass at any moment. They've got to see you be on the knife's edge.

e.r. *You're talking about experiencing the aliveness?*

e.h. That's why we sweat blood in rehearsing all the time. People come up to us and say, ''Oh, Mr. Hawkins, are you just improvising?'' I'm very patient, and say, ''No, we want to show the beauty through form of what we have experienced when we are composing the dance and the music. We want to recall that, on the knife's edge, for you.'' We can miss it, but then, when all the factors are right, the performance takes on an electricity. Sometimes the people backstage are unkind and cause many problems, and don't foster your quietness. I have even had to go over gently and tell the stage men to be quiet just before the curtain goes up, so that I can summon up all my existence, body and soul, into the split second. I can't be diverting my attention.

Now, don't get me wrong, I've had to perform through thick and thin. Once, the percussion instruments were on something unstable and fell in the wings. Another time, an object fell from the flies, and you go right through and don't let anything bother you. But, that's not the moment when your attention is at its peak for that deep stillness which is so necessary to a performance. That's why when people sometimes come late into the theatre, they just might break a moment of deep silence that the dancer or the music might be doing. If you want intensity, you have to pay a little price for it. Well, that's a long spiel.

e.r. *Yes. Thank you very much.*

Summer, 1979

e.r. *Mr. Hawkins, what new works have you created since we last spoke?*

e.h. We did *Greek Dreams with Flute* in '73; that premiered at the Guggenheim Museum in New York City.

e.r. *I know. I couldn't get in, it was so crowded.*

e.h. Then, in '74, *Meditations on Orpheus*, with music by Alan Hovhaness; *Death is the Hunter*, music by Virgil Thomson; and *Parson Weems and the Cherry Tree*. I had the idea for *Parson Weems* about twenty years ago, but it took me a long time to work it out. It's a comic idea, but without any cruelty. I worked very hard and carefully so that the jokes would be jokes about the human condition, and not make fun of anybody. So, I'm very proud of that dance.

e.r. *I thought the costumes were whimsical.*

e.h. I worked for six years on the costumes for *Parson Weems*. One whole set was done in cloth. I chucked them out; they weren't witty, and they were too cumbersome. We had to start all over again. The ones we use now are done in paper. It took me a long time to find people to make the paper wigs and costumes. For example, my costume as a clown, with the red tights and those paper strips, is not something that you arrive at in two minutes. That took an awful lot of experimentation. Once in a while, though, I'll tear one of those strips by being in the wrong movement. And George Washington and the Parson's coats have to be made over every time. The dancers crush and tear them. But that fragility is part of their immediacy. They're not something fixed in a museum that you don't use.

e.r. *Once you've the design, you make them up again?*

e.h. Yes, we have a pattern. Aesthetically, I think *Parson Weems* is very elegant. It's humorous, and yet there isn't any use of junk or cheapness for laughs. I learned that all the accoutrements in a comedy piece could be beautiful and funny from seeing a performance of two comic dances done by a Japanese group some years ago. I was impressed because it was the first time that I saw dances that were comic, but at the same time visually exquisite. That taught me a lesson.

e.r. *Did you work with Virgil Thomson's music from the start of* Parson Weems?

e.h. It took me about two years to persuade him to write the music. I gave him a scenario to write from, and the general length of time. Then he wrote the score. I had to embody the music in the movements. I changed a couple of spots, but it's pretty much according to the scenario.

e.r. *What's your latest dance, and what are you working on now?*

e.h. *Plains Daybreak* is the newest work; it's one of the happiest works that I've ever done. Alan Hovhaness did the music for that. He lives in Seattle and had come to San Francisco to see us perform. I said, "Why don't you write a piece?" And he did. The music has some of the loveliest melodies that you could ask for. The dance opens with the sound of a bass clarinet melody before the dancers come on. I think this melody is as beautiful as the flute theme of the Elysian Fields in Gluck's *Orpheus*. All the melodies are exquisite.

I've been ready to perform *Plains Daybreak* for about a year-and-a-half. The masks took months to do. I think they're probably the most original masks that we've done. There are eight different masks of animals: buffalo, porcupine, antelope, coyote . . . and then, I'm first man. In a way, *Plains Daybreak* was a way of using these beautiful animal masks, and making dances that were like the animals. There's one duet that a man does with the buffalo mask. It's not representational. You see the horns, and the costume is a big square of felt. That dance is a poetic idea of the relation of a man and a buffalo. And the porcupine, for example, evokes the feeling of the porcupine walking or moving. Once I had the image of the mask and the quills, then, somehow, I found the strangeness of that metaphor of the animal moving. It made a charming dance, but it's still a human dancing.

We did the first performance of *Plains Daybreak* in the University in Cincinnati. I don't want this to sound boastful, but the assistant to the sponsor and several other people came up, and said, "Erick this is the most beautiful dance I've ever seen." Visually, with the masks it is lovely.

e.r. *And your newest work?*

e.h. The new piece that I'm doing is totally different. It's with a composer from Los Angeles who's not well known, but he's solid. What he did for me, I think, is going to be very theatrical. I had him write a monolithic score, twenty-one minutes long, and I gave him no idea. I knew the area of his music, and so I said, "You just write a beautiful piece, and I will make a structure to it." The idea for this piece is the invention of the shapes of movement, and I hope to make it quite brilliant.

e.r. *And how long have you been working on it?*

e.h. For about ten days, but I've had the music for nine months.

e.r. *How long does it usually take to finish a piece?*

e.h. It hinges. I'll be able to work faster on this dance than on *Plains Daybreak*. I was working on the actual movement for that piece on and off for a year, but I want to finish this one in five weeks time.

e.r. *Is it for a group?*

e.h. Yes, for eight dancers. I'm not going to be in this one, so that's all the more reason that I can move a little faster. Though, lately, I'm coming up with another comic idea. It's a seed that's been there, but it's kind of crystallized. Maybe I'll do that after this one is completed.

e.r. *Do you think audiences are catching up with your poetry, your still-ness, and the way that you work? I was reading through what* Dance Magazine *said in its 1979 award to you, that ". . . you reached the mystery of the inner imagination." That's a place people forget.*

e.h. I think there's a change. I don't know if it's going to change fast enough for me to be totally happy, and have the money I need to proceed the way I need to without always being so anxious about whether I can go on. I'm hoping that I can keep going and produce the work, and that I'll be a magnet to draw those people who have it in their spirits to respond, even if they don't know whether it's there or not.

As a society, I think we've forgotten something that I mentioned not long ago in a speech down at the Smithsonian, when I said that ''we've forgotten the tender ware.'' That is, the events that come from being inside our actions and experiences. But the response of audiences? For instance, there's a review from Nashville that says that at the end of *Parson Weems*, the audience stood up. I think a large part of the audience has been running, and when they see that something that's poetic doesn't have to be too grim, they permit themselves to relax and enjoy a lighthearted touch.

e.r. Lords of Persia *was the first piece that I saw your company perform. I thought it was wonderful and I still love it. Another of your dances,* Black Lake, *comes to my mind, and of course that has a different sensibility. I remember when I first saw* Black Lake, *I had to concentrate in another way. It was almost like watching a dream, like seeing something flow out of time and space. It was really quite an extraordinary experience for me, in the audience.*

e.h. It's a different idea. After all, *Lords of Persia* is a piece in which men make a metaphor of an actual polo game. In *Black Lake*, all the dancers are metaphors of something that can't be in the human body. It opens with the girl in the red dress and orange mask, and those colors are a metaphor of the main colors that we might associate with a brilliant sunset. Then the metaphor is carried further, because how can those movements of hers convey anything about the setting sun? But some poetic instinct makes people feel *this* movement or *that* one can somehow be associated with the brilliance of the sun. Now getting to that far removed relationship of human movements and natural phenomena is very tricky, very inward. How would you do a dance, for example, as the comet in *Black Lake*? That's something that you see up in the sky, but how do you get someone to do that? I used the metaphor of the long trains on her hair, because that's what ''comet'' means, ''long hair.'' You see the human vitality of the dancer dancing, but what makes it valid is that it's a metaphor. I think that this idea of using metaphor in this way is a unique aspect in contemporary dance. Everyone senses that I'm different, and I think one of the reasons is that I've hit on the use of metaphor. It's that kind of poetic sense that children have. Then like many things, as people grow up, they tend to lose that innocence. I think it would be the height of intensity to reawaken the poetic sense and come back to an innocence.

I'm just hoping that for the good of everybody's happiness, people would learn to see the world poetically. I think that when people stay in the aesthetic dimension they also solve a great many human relations and ethical problems. I think that when somebody sees a work of art or something in nature, without trying to own it or dominate it, see it only for its own sake, then I think their soul is pacified, and they're nicer to the next guy.

e.r. *I saw the overwhelming power of nature in some films of volcanoes at the Museum of Natural History. Those earth-shaking eruptions were so beyond anyone's control, they made me feel my own fears were absurd. That it is nature which really has the last word.*

e.h. You were full of wonder at it.

e.r. *I had never seen anything quite like those films. I think it's those feelings that you want to evoke.*

e.h. I think that when people can see the world without that grubbiness of personal reactions, that's what I mean by the aesthetic dimension, they live and let live more. For me, the people who are aesthetically alert are, in general, nicer people. Otherwise, people who don't get to that are either boorish, which means then that they're insensitive to other people in some way, or else, they get so involved in their own hopes and fears that they become cruel. They just can't let go.

e.r. *The last time we spoke, you mentioned the American Indians when you were talking about metaphor. Has your feeling for nature been influenced by their art?*

e.h. It's true that I've done many dances based on a metaphor from nature, and I want to do more. My early years were spent near the American Southwest. I was born in a little town called Trinidad, Colorado, which is at the bottom of Colorado. It's the dividing line between the Plains Indian culture and the Southwest Indian culture. The mountains are to the north, the plains to the east, and to the south is the Rio Grande River, and the Zuni, Hopi, and Navajo tribes. One summer, early in my dance career, I took an old car and traveled around the area, camping out, in order to see all the Indian ceremonies. It was important because I wanted to see a place where dance was used, not as entertainment or show business, not as virtuosity, but as one aspect of an expression of the total outer and inner world of a people. It was important to me to see grown men dancing and using their bodies in a serious way; and not as though they were some sort of a trained poodle. It was a way of bringing a kind of balance in my own heart of knowing that I wasn't such a fool to try and make dancing my work. Also, the Indians have never felt any alienation from nature. And in some of the dances that I've done, we've been pretty bare. It was just another way of showing how beautiful the body is, and there's nothing negative about it, nothing unworthy about it.

e.r. Is your company planning any performances during the year?

e.h. This summer we may be going to Italy, and we have some dates for next year. We don't have as many as I wish we had, but there are many people who have the notion that dance has to be overt entertainment all the time. If you put that idea of superficial entertainment on all the other arts; poetry, painting, or music, our deep art expression wouldn't exist. I think the better the art is, the more entertaining it is, in the real sense of that word. What is usually called pure entertainment can be fun, but it's like eating some kind of ready-whip. You haven't eaten anything when you've eaten it. Sure, you might think I'm having a great time eating this big, gobbly sundae, but your brain knows you've not been nourished, that you've been kidding yourself.

We'd have more dates if people would gamble on the fact that audiences would be stimulated by us. We did one performance up at Jamestown, New York, and the Arts Council man said, "I don't think there's ever been a modern dance concert in this town of Jamestown." After, the review said, "Delightful, beautiful," and so forth, and he was pleased. We have to have enough guts to keep going, and there have to be enough people who will book us.

e.r. Do you give workshops?

e.h. Yes. Sometimes the lectures and lecture-demonstrations are useful. There are many people who come to watch dance, but who haven't any real notion about either what is possible, or what is desirable. Until that can get sorted out, they're not quite sure how to let themselves react to dance events. It's a process of continuing education. To enjoy anything, there's no ending; you have to get into the fine points. If you're going to watch a game, and you don't know the rules of the game and the fine points, then you won't know where the players excel. Part of a game is different from a performance, but some part of it is the same. You're watching the human spirit use its full power.

The Erick Hawkins Dance Company is appearing in Woodstock, a community two hours north of New York City. I travel there in order to see *Plains Daybreak*, Erick's most recent work because it is uncertain when this dance will be performed in a New York theatre. Arriving in time for the matinee, I notice a sprinkling of children mixed in with the local audience. Mostly they are quiet and absorbed throughout the afternoon, but now and then a young voice breaks into the performing tension to ask "Why did he drop that?" or "What was he doing?" only to be answered by a whisper and a quick hush. Except for these disarming moments, the audience is attentive, and the congenial atmosphere gives a feeling of intimacy rarely found in a New York City theatre. In fact, I find the country setting both inside and outside the Woodstock Playhouse an appropriate background for viewing *Plains Daybreak*, since its basic theme is a gentle look at man's relationship to nature.

As the dance begins, a foggy haze permeates the stage, lightly encompassing its bare spaces in an eerie, expectant mood. Two round globes with the cold, stony look of planets seen from afar hang from the proscenium above, while in between these sculptured images of the moon and the sun dangle a handful of twinkling stars. Soon, a melancholy, melodic phrase floats slowly into the air. Then light replaces the foggy haze, the twinkling stars multiply, the bassoon sings, and the audience waits for the dancers to make their first entrance. But the stage remains empty.

After those first silent moments of *Plains Daybreak*, an assortment of wonderful animals fills the barren space. There is a buffalo, an antelope, a porcupine, a hawk, a fish, a snake, and a raccoon. On the dancer-wearers' heads are imaginative headpieces, each a work of visual exquisiteness recalling the physical appearance of the animal. My favorite, the porcupine, has a shaky head of rattling spokes, a long quill in its back, and wiggly feet.

Alone and in groups these dancer-animals amble or lope across that void of space which we know to be the earth but see more immediately as the stage. Then into this world of unique beings comes a man, who stands erect but is at first just another variation of a visual form—for he, too, wears a symbolic headpiece. But the source of this dance is our world of reality, and the man, a strong, charismatic Erick Hawkins, must use his bow and arrow to stalk the buffalo. No longer does the beautiful, solo oboe speak of the mystery of the void. A drum and cello overwhelm the lyric sound with the percussive drama of the hunt. And the beauty of each being is subordinated to the struggle for survival.

I find it surprising that Erick's theatre dance is such a symbolic world of visual beauty. Because of his constantly aware verbal analysis of thoughts and feelings, I would have guessed that his choreography would also reflect a strong, literal sensibility. Instead, most of his dances are abstract, with little or no direct storytelling and a minimum of recognizable gestures. As in *Plains Daybreak*, there is always a floating quality to the dancers' movements, and a careful balancing of the visual and aural elements. Erick always works closely with the artist who designs the sets, costumes, and the often-used symbolic masks, and the composer who writes the score for the dance. In this instance, Ralph Lee is credited with the designs and Alan

Hovahnnes with the music; the entire concept, however, originates with Erick and reflects his poetic vision.

Watching this afternoon's performance, I see an Erick Hawkins I have never known. The suble optimism of *Plains Daybreak* reveals someone who refuses to be overwhelmed by the unsettling implications of the nature of existence, and I hadn't realized that Erick's strength ran so deep. I no longer feel, as I did when watching him teach a class at the school, that I am recycling my past, but instead that this added dimension enlarges my understanding of Erick as a person, and as a dance-maker.

The afternoon's program comes to an end with a colorful storybook dance, *Parson Weems and the Cherry Tree*. With its ingenious costumes, this delightful piece has the look of pages torn from a nineteenth-century child's history primer. Only this make-believe dance is a farcical retelling of American history in which a gentle Lucifer/clown figure undermines the great historical figure of George Washington through a series of mischievous adventures. It's a humorous, ironic dance of almost mimed storytelling, set to a cocky musical score by Virgil Thomson, and very different from Erick's other works. Most surprising to me is Erick's own performance as the clown figure. I have always pictured him as someone too dignified to act the part of a clown, but he is very convincing in his role as an amusing prankster.

After the performance I go backstage. Erick greets me with a friendly "Hello, I'm glad that you could come," while removing the long, red nose he wears for his stage role. He is still dressed in his outlandish costume of billowing white paper strips, and I feel that I'm speaking to someone who at this moment is between two lives, that of a fictional stage character and that of the day-to-day person. Erick next takes off his odd, red wig with the long, upturned pigtail, and once the wig is removed he assumes his habitual demeanor. The afternoon's performance is uppermost in his mind, and after giving detailed comments about their work to the dancers, he states in a definitive, emphatic tone to the backstage visitors, "The dancers are inspired by that animal heat projected by the audience. There's nothing like it. It brings the dancers to the focus of a performance tension, to that very intense peak."

I say goodbye to Erick and to the dancers who stand idly in the wings, unraveling their performing energy. They have another program to dance this evening and must prepare for the second show between performances. I would have enjoyed seeing another program and regret that I haven't made plans to stay on. The afternoon's performance has been unusual, however, with a special gentle quality, and I am pleased that there has been this opportunity of seeing the Erick Hawkins Dance Company in such a relaxed atmosphere. I finally leave the Woodstock Playhouse and start my return trip to New York City. On my way home, I realize that not only has the afternoon's dancing left me with a smile on my face, but I no longer find Erick Hawkins such an overpowering personality. I'm not sure how this has happened. But I know that somehow, it had to do with seeing *Plains Daybreak*. This piece extended my insight and my understanding of Erick's work, and with these new perceptions, I crossed an old barrier, erected by my own youthful timidity.

Keeping Up with
Merce Cunningham

That is what dancing is about, looking at something.

QUITE BY ACCIDENT I discovered Merce Cunningham's classes in the summer of 1952. Mine is not so much a conscious decision to switch from Graham to Cunningham as a matter of chance and my own schedule. But modern dance is extremely partisan about such allegiances, and when I introduce myself before the first class, I tell Merce in a confessional tone of voice that my previous training has been at the Graham school. Merce reacts to my admission with an amused smile and says nothing. In the course of the summer, he surprises me by unexpectedly remarking, "You're more lyrical than most of those who've studied with Martha." I take his comment as a compliment and it endears Merce to me forever.

A small group of eight students attend a daily class in the loft Merce uses as a dance studio. In our late teens or early twenties, we are all serious about dance and self-absorbed in our own progress. The class starts around noon, the hottest part of the day, but unmindful of the heat we each make our way to Eighth Street, climb the stairs, and change our clothes in a makeshift dressing room off in a corner of the studio-loft. Ready, we take our places in the studio where Merce waits. Warm-ups start in a standing position: bodies erect, feet parallel, arms down. On Merce's count, we go over, pulsing front to the center . . . then up . . . to the side . . . up . . . to the other side . . . like figures in an animated geometric drawing. About half-an-hour after the class begins, we sweat so profusely from the midday heat that one by one we reach for our towels to wipe our faces dry. Merce wraps his towel around his neck, prizefighter style. Otherwise he remains as seemingly unaffected by the intense heat as by anything else that might or might not happen.

Our class is often visited by the two cats who belong to the dancer who owns the loft. The cats meander through the hole of a partitioning wall and then saunter across the floor near the barre on the back wall. On Merce's advice, we let them go their own way and continue our work as if they aren't there. And Merce is right; we never overstep each other's territory.

Merce's soft, unhurried voice both directs and accompanies our work throughout the class. He also demonstrates each exercise, and as the combinations progress in complexity, I am so impressed by his graceful, elegant movements that I copy him as closely as I can, like a child under the spell of the Pied Piper. I hope to absorb Merce's deft, nochalant style.

The summer days go on and so do we. One day in the midst of a hot spell so unbearable that offices and factories close early, Merce encourages us with one of his casual understatements that so easily define a problem. "People cope with hot weather in various ways. For dancers it's good for stretching muscles. You can develop a very deep plié in this weather and that's important. The Japanese, you know . . ." Aside from the weather, the other constant topic of conversation centers on a large, freestanding blackboard with musical notations jotted on it. In answer to questions, Merce explains the meaning of these symbols and figures. "John Cage and I are working on some musical/time theories. He is exploring the differences between Eastern and Western scales, and the effect they have on music and movement." I'm fascinated by these bits of aesthetic musings, and many years later I remember Merce's comments when I see his dance company perform. But by that time, Merce had left those blackboard conversations far behind in his search for aesthetic guidelines.

When the summer ends, I return to college. I don't see Merce Cunningham for two years, until I again take classes with him in his latest studio, an old gym on Sheridan Square in Manhattan's West Village. My dance loyalties, I find, are still divided. An invisible cord ties me to the Graham school, though I have personal feelings about the second-hand atmosphere of the classes there. Few of the teachers can transcend Martha Graham's strong personality, yet her words and manner are dutifully imitated. In contrast, I find the simplicity of the classes given by Cunningham, the curly-haired man with the impish smile and the quiet, even, low-keyed personality, a refreshing experience.

Little in the technique Merce teaches us resembles the Graham patterns of exercises and movements. A Graham class starts on the floor and the body is warmed up through a number of exercises that develop the focal Graham dynamic of contraction and release. With Merce, we always begin in a standing position, even during the first moments of the class, and the initial focus revolves around making our spines malleable. There is a peripheral similarity between Merce's pulsating spine and Graham's contraction-release, as both utilize a fluid spine; but the physical beginnings in the body are entirely different. In addition, the motor dynamic of a Graham contraction-release is a force that is used often to express an emotional connotation, while the pulsating spine Merce works with is just that, a pulsating, fluid spine that is the physical center of the body.

Merce is an attentive, purposeful teacher who makes the work seem simple: we have muscles, bones, a head, torso, spine, arms, hands, fingers, legs, feet, toes, and we move them separately, together, in an infinite variety of combinations. It seems easy, until Merce demonstrates a combination for the students to copy. They do; but what he does with ease and

The curly haired man with the impish smile and the quiet, even, low-keyed personality. Merce Cunningham (Photo: Lois Greenfield)

grace they do laboriously and awkwardly. It takes time to develop strength and control over our bodies, something that many of us in the class must still do, but there is something else. Somehow, the unique personality of each individual is revealed through his or her own moving body. Technique provides the discipline and a form to mask the barest idiosyncrasies, but the essence of a person's spirit gives an individual quality to the physical presence. Sometimes a personality transforms itself, through dance, into a form of beauty. Merce is one of these people and it is very much in evidence as he carefully demonstrates the simplest patterns to his students.

The next time I see Merce, a decade has gone by and he and his dance company are startling London with a series of performances. I'm in London, on my way to resettle in New York City after living abroad for many years. I am both surprised and delighted when I read that the Merce Cunningham Dance Company will be giving a week of performances at the Sadlers Wells Theatre, for in all the years since I first took class with Merce in that Eighth Street studio, I've never seen any of his theatre performances.

That 1964 London season is a success for Merce and his company. The London dance world is fascinated and general interest runs high enough for the company to continue its summer run at the Phoenix Theatre in New York. My own experience is confusing, for I go with great anticipation and come away with a sense of bewilderment. I'm so shocked by the taut expression aging Merce's face that it unnerves me. It's an instance of life having more power than art, for I'm as affected by this physical change that came far too early as I am by the evening's program. Little of that night's dancing remains in my memory; only bits and pieces from *Antic Meet*: Merce crossing the stage with a chair strapped to his back, and that's mystifying; Merce playing around with a multi-sleeved sweater, and that's amusing; Merce in white overalls doing a sort of soft-shoe dance, and that's delightful. But during most of the program I keep visualizing Merce as he looked the last time I saw him, in his Sheridan Square studio.

During the 1960's and 1970's, Merce Cunningham is acknowledged as the major influence in American contemporary dance. He is the spearhead of the avant-garde movement, and many young dancers are influenced by his ideas on both movement and aesthetics. Merce's use of chance as an integral part of his choreography is discussed, analyzed, and copied, becoming a modish idea that is still popular. For me, it's an echo of those conversations around the blackboard in the summer of 1952, since that was an early step in developing the underlying philosophical structure for Merce's choreography. I think the act of dancing is the primary aspect of his work, but the aesthetic principles influence his choice of collaborators and his method of structuring a work.

Over the years, Merce has collaborated with many contemporary composers, musicians, painters, sculptors, and designers. Collaboration is an overall term that defines a working relationship that is usually an association of two or more people working together on one project. The implication is that they work together to create one idea. In a loose sense this is what happens when Merce Cunningham works with his collaborators on one of his dance pieces. But instead of defining the parts—the dance, the music, the set, the costumes, the lighting—as one, Merce chooses his collaborators, sets some specific elements like the length of time or the mood of the dance, and then each person works out his or her own individual vision. Finally, at the dress rehearsal, the parts are brought together and what emerges can be strikingly cohesive, as in the dances *Rain Forest* and *Summerspace*.

Merce has continued to work with John Cage since their first association in 1942, but he also has worked with many other contemporary composers, including David Behrman, Earle Brown, David Tudor, and Christian Wolff. Among the many contemporary visual artists who have worked with the Cunningham Company are Andy Warhol, Frank Stella, Richard Lippold, Sonja Sekula, Remy Charlip, Robert Rauschenberg, and others. So many contemporary composers and artists have been commissioned to work for the Merce Cunningham Dance Company that their collaboration has been likened to the period when Diaghiliev found Stravinsky, Ravel, Picasso, Cocteau, and other contemporary artists of the period to work with his Ballet Russe.

I begin to appreciate the clear poetry of Merce's choreography during the Cunningham Company's 1970 appearance at the Brooklyn Academy of Music. At first, the overall clarity of the dancers' movements in ballets like *Place, Scramble*, and *How To Pass, Kick, Fall, and Run* remind me of contemporary abstract painting. The Cunningham dances have the same architectural sense of space and profound simplicity. And the dance pieces create an atmosphere of mood through the play of similar forces such as dynamics, design, and color.

I discover, too, that surprise is a recurring element in Cunningham's work. Movement patterns, staging, and concept are totally unpredictable from the audience's point of view; partly, I think, because of Merce's own puckish sense of humor, and partly because of his use of chance in plotting the dances. Eventually, after seeing the company dance on different occasions, I move away from associating the dance pieces with anything other than their own presentation. An evening of Cunningham dancing is hard work, because there is no story line, no characterization, no sequential pattern or movement as a handle for bringing the dance work into an aspect of associative meaning. The technique of the dancers is obviously important to the complexity of their movements, but unlike the classical ballet, the dancers do not exploit their technique as a thrilling feat to the accompaniment of beautifully melodic, rhythmic music. No, the Cunning-

ham work is its own poetry that frees the imaginative experience and
extends it beyond a verbal experience through the force of our basic
kinesthetic sense.

Merce's own dancing remains eloquent. He is less capable of virtuosity,
but as articulate as he was when I first saw him in 1952. Over the years, my
admiration for his purposefulness and his idealism has grown with my
appreciation of the difficulties he faces in order to continue his work. In
1970, the Brooklyn Academy of Music offers Merce something that had
been impossible for him to realize in all these years, a regular New York
season.

I arrange to speak to Merce at his school, located in an old loft on Third
Avenue and Thirty-Third Street, about the residency program. Arriving
early, I'm invited to watch a class until Merce is free. I find it a sentimental
and exhilarating experience. Seeing the dancers work in the studio, I'm
reminded how subtly the Cunningham technique channels energy and
weight.

When Merce is ready, we go into an empty classroom to tape our conversation. It's difficult at first, since Merce prefers to say as little as
possible, even to ex-students—he's had so many. But seeing the look of
consternation on my face, he expands his initial yes/no answers into the
conversation that follows.

*e.r. Mr. Cunningham, yours is a name long known to the dance world.
Now, with the regular seasons at the Brooklyn Academy of Music, a
more general public will have a chance to discover your superb dancing and choreography. It's clear that the audience is going to benefit,
but will the regular seasons benefit you as well?*

m.c. Oh, certainly. The Brooklyn Academy of Music has one of the best
dance stages in the country. The physical setup for dancing is simply
superb.

e.r. Why is that? What makes a good stage?

m.c. If I'm going to work on a proscenium stage, then I prefer one which
has the space that the Academy has, and also one that has its
backstage possibilities. The setup for dancing also includes a situation
for the orchestra, or the musicians, or whatever. I don't use a large
orchestra, but the space is there, just the same. The auditorium is
visually adequate for people who are seated; the sight lines are good.
So everyone, or almost everyone, can see very well. And since that's
what dancing is about, looking at something, it's very nice that the
audience can watch it easily. As a theatre, the opera house is really
marvelous.

*e.r. What is the effect of knowing that you're to have two regular seasons
in the New York area? Will that influence your planning of works?*

m.c. It just makes more work. It's a question of time. I, myself, like
working on dances very much, but with more time taken up with

performing, both in Brooklyn and touring, less time can be given to making new pieces. It calls for a juggling act between the two. I'm delighted that people want to come and see us—it has nothing to do with that. But there's only so much time, and if 50 percent is spent here, you have to give way someplace else. That's all.

e.r. *When you're not performing at the Academy, you'll tour?*

m.c. Wc travel across America; and also toured in Europe last summer for two months, June and July. All that simply takes up time, plus having the school with classes going on here in Manhattan every day. But I'd really like to say that the Brooklyn Academy has done wonderful things, not just for dancing, but for theatre in general in New York. Mr. Lichtenstein [the director] is expanding the Academy in many different directions. He's been superb with dancers, allowing so many different ones to perform, besides opening the Academy to the Living Theatre and other theatre groups. All that seems to me to have enlivened the New York scene. He's been very concerned with letting things be seen which are not ordinarily seen, and letting them be seen in good circumstances.

e.r. *Are you preparing any new works for this year?*

m.c. Yes. Hopefully. Well, I've a new one that we did in Paris in June, which hasn't yet been seen in New York. We'll offer it in our season in November, and I'm also working on another now.

e.r. *Does your company stay with you from year to year?*

m.c. I've had a company for a number of years. By that, I don't mean the same dancers, of course, but I have, with or without funds, simply tried over the past fifteen years to have a dance organization. That meant that I constantly gave classes, and then quite as constantly, rehearsed something, for one performance or for a season, it made no difference. In recent years, through the generosity of various foundations, there have been grants from the government and private individuals, easing some of the money problems which for so many years were simply monumental.

e.r. *I realize that.*

m.c. That's always true for dancing, because it's expensive. You want to have dancers around to dance, but they have to be paid. But, I think, there has been a great opening in the last few years, all due to McLuhan's idea about the visual world. People can look at dancing now, and not think they have to worry about understanding it or enjoying it. Through television, people have become more accustomed to relating to a visual image; since dance is visual, it's not such a desperate effort for them any more. It's not so forbidding, and so people are interested.

e.r. *And do you think that is why the audience for dance has grown so much in the past few years?*

m.c. I think dancing is sharing in that. Dancing isn't causing it, but it's sharing in all of this shift. It must be something like that, since the audiences for dancing have changed so radically in the, say, past five years. It's not just here in New York, it's all over the United States, and abroad too. That growth in audiences is, in turn, producing more interest on the dancer's part. Both forces work together. The dancers are inspired to create more works and to explore in different ways. All that, I think, adds to the increased appreciation of the dance.

In 1974, Merce Cunningham, newly settled into his large, airy Westbeth studio, starts a series of performances called "events." These are fragments and sequences of new and old dances that are scrambled together and performed to an unpredictable score, arranged for the evening by a specially invited composer. Though Merce Cunningham's Dance Company has performed for years in gymnasiums and other nontraditional dance spaces, the ideas for these events grew out of an appearance at a Viennese museum because a title was needed to advertise their performance. Merce suggested calling it "Museum Event." When the European tour ended and the Company returned to New York, Merce began to present evenings of dance events. He gives each event a number instead of a name, and uses these hour-long, no-intermission dance concerts to further experiment with the juxtaposition of a variety of movement sequences, time sequences, and television images.

At one of these events, a man sings the sounds of a John Cage score. It's a grating, irritating sound; an inarticulate, human voice that has been electronically amplified into a shrill, rhythmic noise. It drones on for over an hour. During this time, Merce and his dancers perform beautiful, austere sequences of movement. And, in one section, Merce builds an unforgettable solo from small, eloquent hand gestures. Standing quietly, his hands slowly cup like the paws of an animal. Opening, Merce's fingers and hands move in a deft pattern of movement speech as if marking a design of battement exercises. A half-walk-half-run takes him to another section of the performing space. He repeats the small patterns until they grow, shuddering through his body. There's a feeling of suppressed energy, outlining a dance that never fully explodes into space. And there's a sad feeling to this dance that Merce performs with such graceful eloquence.

Expectations of small audiences, high costs, and general lack of interest in discovering contemporary dance keep Merce Cunningham from bringing his dance company into a Broadway theatre until 1972. Finally, the growing popularity of dance makes such a season feasible. On the opening night, Merce is awarded an artistic citation from the City of New York, applauding him for his visionary work. Since Merce has traveled with his

Merce Cunningham and members of his company in **Squaregame** *(Photo: Lois Greenfield)*

company all over the world during the last twenty-five years, while struggling for New York seasons, he responds to the presentation with an odd,
wry story. "John Cage was driving somewhere when he was stopped by a
cop. He was driving too fast or something like that. The policeman told
John that he was going to give him a citation. John said, 'Thank you very
much'—and I thank *you* very much."

With the help and interest of a number of leading artists and the presence
of Vice-President Mondale's wife, Joan Mondale, the Cunningham Company is able to organize a return New York season in 1978. During this run
at the City Center, a popular dance theatre that has recently begun to
welcome modern dance companies, *Inlets*, a work new to New York, is
premiered and instantly becomes my favorite Cunningham dance piece. It
is one of Merce Cunningham's collaborative works that, like the earlier
Rain Forest, come together in a magic wholeness. Cunningham's classically simple choreography is, by chance, juxtaposed against the sensuous
images and sounds of nature. The mood is somber as a glowing moon
gleams through a transparent scrim curtain. The dancers, seen through this
shadowy fabric, are busy with their dancing. At first the scrim acts as an
illusory shadow; it's an introductory veil that will lift, revealing the dancers in a clear, open light. But the scrim never lifts and the dancers remain
isolated, practicing their simple, stark balances, leaps, rolls, and jumps,
while the air is filled with the rustling sound of pinecones and the whisper-
ing of water in conch-shells. The moon, descending, ends its voyage across
the stage. In the audience, there are some who understand and are en-
thralled by the poetic, elusive tension of Cunningham's understated dance
statement. There are others who have not grown along with the Cunningham Company, and during intermission, they are the ones who ask, "What
does it mean?"

There is always a disproportionately large number of dancers at performances of the Merce Cunningham Dance Company. In fact, someone, not
a dancer, took a look at the parading audience during an intermission at a
City Center performance and remarked, "I've never seen an audience so
erect, with such beautiful posture." Dancers are there not only because
many have studied with Merce and follow his work, but also because, with
their highly developed sense of empathetic movement, they understand
what the Cunningham Company is doing.

Much of modern dance's early support came from college dance de-
partments. Often under the aegis of physical education, modern dance was
introduced to hundreds of students as part exercise, part art. In spite of the
administrative confusion about the validity of dance as an art form, many
students took modern dance seriously and either pursued careers associated with dance or formed a nucleus of loyal audience support. The

college network also laid the groundwork for the development of such programs as the National Endowment's Dance Touring Program which underwrites workshops, performances, and residency programs in colleges and communities throughout the United States.

In recent years, college dance teachers have formed the American Dance Guild, an organization which serves their professional needs. Their 1979 award goes to Merce Cunningham and is presented to him at a special dinner during the American Dance Guild's June conference in Washington, Dance In Transition, Issues for the '80's. When Merce arrives at the Holiday Inn banquet room, the audience stands and greets him with a warm ovation. Merce, looking lean and elegant in street clothes, smiles his appreciation and then shakes the hands of the teachers who line up to meet him personally and to offer their congratulations.

As an important creative force in the field, Merce Cunningham stands apart, somewhat as a remote hero figure, in the lives of these dance teachers. Even though everyone in the room shares a lifetime of involvement with the art of dance, there's an unstated but acknowledged gulf between those who are the creative fountainhead of the art and those who serve it as acolytes. Merce does his best to bridge this gap and share his understanding of everyone's work and their personal dedication to the dance. For him, the will to survive is the key to staying with the art. As Merce begins his acceptance speech, he illustrates this feeling at first with a John Cage story and then with his own recollections.

The thought of John Cage's brazenness gives Merce a chuckle as he begins to tell of his friend's idiosyncratic cooking habits, which created a commotion in one European hotel; but instead of being chucked out of the hotel, Cage maneuvered himself into the kitchen as a chef. Then speaking of his own efforts at survival, he reminisces, "Once, years ago, I wasn't very well and I went to my doctor and he took care of me. As I was leaving, I said, 'Thank you doctor for curing me.' He answered, 'Don't thank me, thank your parents for a good constitution.' I've been thinking of that moment because that may be one of the things that you need to survive in dance. Though there's something about dancing, that if you love it enough, it helps you to survive."

There's an appreciative round of applause and some murmuring in the room. Merce goes on in his soft voice, "We [Merce Cunningham and Dance Company] just came back from a five week tour in France, Germany, and Holland. We were in some marvelous theatres and some that were not so marvelous; but, each time, I thought, 'Here's a chance again. Maybe I'll find out something that I didn't know before.' It doesn't matter whether it's little or big, but each time the process has to be like a spring rather than like something that's been fixed. And I think dance is something that not only changes, but also remains something you can deal with each day. It's not something that you figured out yesterday and then you sort of repeat it, or whatever. But, dance can become something new each day. At least, that's always been my thinking. I've thought, here's a new chance with each new day, and I have the same feeling when we perform.''

Merce's words are appreciated for he has touched on many common problems. Staying with dance becomes a way of life, and over the years it can be both taxing and grueling: the monetary compensation falls below the general salary scale, and there are many sceptics, especially in an academic situation, who challenge the teaching of dance as a valid subject. The end of his speech brings another round of strong applause, which is a genuine, heartfelt response.

Soon after the speeches, another line forms for the self-service buffet. Later, after everyone has eaten, David Vaughan, the Cunningham archivist, entertains us with some old theatrical songs. Merce enjoys the singing, and when David finishes, the Cunningham contingent gathers their things in time to get the last shuttle back to New York City.

Discovering Alwin Nikolais

Doll, you forget, we are already in outer space.

M Y BELATED INTRODUCTION TO Alwin Nikolais's dance theatre world came in 1969, years after hearing it described in tantalizing words. His work, I had been told, involved a startling use of light, electronic sound, and visual effects. In fact, it was common dance knowledge that long before mixed media emerged as a novelty in the discotheques, Nikolais, or "Nik," as he is often called, was exploring the possibilities of unconventional lighting at his Henry Street Settlement House headquarters in Manhattan. Finally, when an opportunity came to view his company, I was more than ready to exchange an evening at home, where I knew what to expect, for an evening at the theatre, where I had only the vaguest idea of what I would see.

I wasn't disappointed, as an evening spent with the Alwin Nikolais Dance Theatre is an incredible theatre experience that cannot be imagined in advance. Never could I have imagined *Somniloquy*, an opulent dream of splendiferous colors melting into shimmering backdrops of amorphous images. It was a hypnotizing montage of lights and electronic sound bringing to mind the shifting of patterns in a slowly turning kaleidoscope. The dancers mingle with the merging and emerging colors, adding a recognizable physical link to this mysterious visual world first created by Nikolais in 1957.

When the curtain goes up on *Imago*, I am introduced to the whimsical images Nikolais loves to put on the stage. Dancers with totally unexpected, inconceivable arm appendages that resemble strange bones, show off their exoticism in a witty, self-examining narcissism. I have to ask myself: How did Nikolais imagine such creatures? Why has he created such a strange aberration of the human form? To judge by the light choreographic touch, these nonsense creatures actually enjoy quivering their legs and flailing their arms about in time to a score of crashing, dissonant noises. I have to ask myself, "Just where do these people come from? Who are they supposed to be?"

In the same mood, but perhaps more amusing, is *Noumenon* from *Masks, Props, and Mobiles*. In this piece, a faceless trio, entirely covered by sacks, comes to life through various patterns of body pulsations. Without fronts, backs, middles, or clearly defined extremities, they remind me of a collection of potato sacks pulled over a mound of bubbling rubber. By this time in the evening's program I can see that Nikolais has indeed created a unique theatre of atmosphere, although it is weirdly poetic in its imagery. But where there's poetry, there's another layer of meaning, and Nikolais does have more on his mind than experimenting with lights and colors. A program note accompanying a new work, *Echo* (1969), mentions that this piece is a statement about the individual in today's abstract cities. While it is edifying to know there's an underlying philosophy behind the work I am seeing, I am intrigued, quite simply, by these extraordinary visions. My introduction to Nikolais's world has a startling effect on my imaginative powers. I find the boundaries of my own limited imagination extended into new vistas by the rapid succession of Nikolais's bewitching images; and the evening's program is only half over.

As *Echo* unfolds, the shifting relationships of bodies, lights, reflections, colors, and sounds affect my familiar perceptions of space. Silhouettes of moving figures appear against a strange forest of trees that are not trees, but arms, then feet turned up, soles to the sky, then moving bodies, then trees. Suddenly lights, colors, and the backdrop become a lemon sky and desert hills. Nothing remains in its own recognizable form for more than an instant and the resulting disorientation of the images on stage has the timeless, spaceless quality of a dream. The sound of mumbling speech is heard, while the dancers move through the shadows. Again the background changes; this time, a lone figure is shadowed against the image of a larger self projected onto the background scenes. Finally, the group is overwhelmed by the huge buildings.

At the evening's end I am left with an impression of having seen a strange, disturbing, but wonderful vision. I realize that to achieve the effects of his unconventional theatre pieces, Nikolais uses a rich interplay of images, including the dancers, but I wondered as I left the theatre, what next? What could Nikolais possibly do after this? What strange forms would he devise, and what phantasmagoric delights would he create in the future with his lights and colors?

New York performances by the Alwin Nikolais Dance Theatre have never been all that frequent, and I have to wait over a year before I again see the company. As I then continue over several seasons to watch the Nikolais Company in their appearances in various New York theatres, City Center, the ANTA Theatre, the Brooklyn Academy of Music, the Beacon Theatre, I find that though the first thrill of discovery has faded, I am still curious to find out what new images Nik can devise. I am never disappointed because he has an imagination that plunges into new realms with all the boundless zeal of a fairy-tale wizard.

On each program there is a divertissement section culled from a variety of works, and in this way I see moments from *Allegory* (1957), *Sanctum* (1964), *Vaudeville of the Elements* (1965), and *Masks, Props and Mobiles*

. . . so calm, so genial, and so unlike a mysterious conjurer of new worlds. Alwin Nikolais (photo: Sandler)

(1953). Perhaps the bone-hooped, striped figures of the trio from *Vaudeville of the Elements*, whose antics defy description, provide the most extraordinary sight of unusual people in Nikolais's repertoire. I do find, however, that as I become familiar with different pieces, these visual spectacles, which at first dazzle with their fantasy images, eventually hang together as an unending epic of one choreographer's view of twentieth-century man. In Nikolais's work, the elements of light, sound, time, space, and man become interdependent for the total effect. Since Nikolais paints the slides, plots the lighting, designs the costumes, creates the electronic sound, and then sets the choreography for all these pieces, his work is more centrally expressive of a personal vision than most theatre or dance performances, which usually involve collaboration among various artists working in different areas.

New audiences are constantly discovering Nikolais's work, as I learned at some recent performances of the company at Manhattan's Beacon Theatre, a converted art deco movie house that has often been used for rock concerts. The program was a combination of works from past years and the new pieces *Styx* and *Triad*. At the last curtain call of the evening, Alwin Nikolais, as is his custom, comes out to take a bow. A large man with white hair and a beaming smile, and glowing with good will, he joins hands with the dancers and comes forward on stage to acknowledge happily the audience's warm reception. I don't know how others feel, but I am always taken aback when Nik comes out to take his bow at the end of a performance. He is always so jovial and delighted, and I, after sitting through the manifestation of his incredible dreams, expect, at the least, a wizard or a demon. I'm not really sure who should be standing there in Nik's place, perhaps a Merlin figure with a high, conical, silver hat perched on a long, pointed face, and wrapped in a huge cape? But then that would be a banal image and Nikolais knows better than to manifest the obvious.

It was the banal though, that finally erased the magician image I had of Alwin Nikolais. Quite unexpectedly, he was a guest at a summer dinner party given by friends. I had never fully expected that Alwin Nikolais would look like one of his own fantasy creatures, but I didn't expect him to be quite so calm, so genial, and so unlike a mysterious conjurer of new worlds. It wasn't the thing to say, and instead, when I was able to speak to Alwin Nikolais, I said, "I've been so intrigued by your work that I'm curious how you came to such an unusual and so personal a concept of dance theatre? Where do you come from?"

Nikolais chuckled a bit in a way that made me certain that he had heard this question any number of times. "I was born in Southington, Connecticut, and I grew up there."

"And," I asked, "did you study dance there?"

"I started with music," answered Nikolais. "Eventually I got a job accompanying silent films in a movie house. You know, the film would roll and someone would provide the background music by playing piano or organ. That's what I was doing. I did a lot of improvising, to match the screen action, but that was my only involvement with motion until I saw a performance of the German modern dancer, Mary Wigman, way back in 1933. That really changed my life. The use of percussion in Wigman's music was just wonderful, and I wanted some information about it for my own musical knowledge. When I went to get it, that was in Hartford, I was talked into studying dance, which I did, and that was many years ago, now."

"Did you study with Mary Wigman?" I asked.

"No," replied Nikolais, "I didn't go to Germany, where Wigman did her teaching, but I did study for many years with a pupil of hers [Truda Kaschmann] in Connecticut. While I was studying dance, I was also, to earn my keep, the director of a marionette theatre. Somehow, I was always involved, from childhood on, in some aspect of theatre. But anyway, perhaps from watching those puppets perform so much, I became involved with the effects of motion versus emotion. That really was it, because by that time, World War II was here and I went into the army. Later, after the War, I studied with Hanya Holm, a Wigman disciple, in New York. Finally, I began working, in 1949, at the Henry Street Settlement House."

Nikolais smiles. That is definitely all. The rest of the evening passes quietly and comfortably. About six months later, I have an opportunity to interview Nikolais for "Dance Focus," and I ask him the rest of the questions that had been on my mind at the summer dinner party.

e.r. *How did you arrive at your individual approach to lighting?*

a.n. Well, the more formal setup in technical theatre was based pretty much on realism with, for example, the old McCandless system of light coming from above to create sunlight and that sort of thing. I wasn't concerned with that kind of natural effect; I was concerned with light as illumination from any source so I developed a kind of three-dimensional lighting. I put a great many lights on the floor—I still do—and from overhead, so that I can control luminosity of the figure from any angle. This was because I wasn't concerned about moonlight or sunlight; I was concerned about design, color design.

e.r. *On the stage?*

a.n. Right there, yes. The same with music; I was concerned with sound. I don't believe that I was always terribly concerned with whether or not the score was a great musical composition. I was very conscious of the necessity of each art's supplying a portion of the whole, but if one part, by itself, supplied everything, then the others were naturally diminished. So that in working with a multimedia scheme you really have to sense how one phase has to diminish to allow the other to take place within the same, you know, pot of stew. And this is of course, why, very often, you hear writers who say, "They don't dance," or "They don't do this." Well, of course, the dancers have to share the thing. I mean, I can't have them do twirling and high kicks and all that sort of thing when I'm very strongly concerned with, let's say, the design on the thigh as the person enters the light; and this we do very carefully.

e.r. *So the movement is really part of that whole world that you're creating on the stage at that moment.*

a.n. Oh, yes.

e.r. *Rather than simply a series of dance movements, let's say.*

a.n. It's not just a free sashaying around in it. It's an ecology of the stage. Rather than dominate, the dances join the grace of all the elements that surround the dancers and of which they are also a part. Thus, they also take part in the universality of environment and not inflict themselves with disgrace upon it, which, I think, is a kind of old-fashioned need in our sociological times, isn't it?

e.r. *At the moment, yes. Are you influenced by your ideas of man and the world when you make your own world in the theatre? For example, you were talking about ecology.*

a.n. These are words that we now know, but that I have felt for some time. Originally, I broke away from the Freudian concepts because I didn't believe that life was wholly the result of a sexually dominated libido. I refused to go along with that, and of course, I tried to reduce this overpowering sexuality so that I could see the human being a little more clearly and not always have him look to me as if he were, you know, on the verge of a make. This also meant redesigning the light in which he moved. Then the story form of boy-meets-girl, and all that sort of thing, didn't interest me because I thought we would learn more about humanity if we placed him in the universe where he belongs.

e.r. *A man among other animals, inhabiting the world.*

a.n. Oh yes, in the universe, not even a world. I remember one man who told me that I'm from outer space. I said, "Doll, you forget, we are already in outer space." But I don't think of myself in terms of Buck Rogers and all that stuff.

e.r. *No, but I think because you've created a whole new look on the stage, in fact, a whole universe, that people then use those adjectives and say your work is spacelike or moonlike. I think because you conjure all of this up that you're sometimes referred to as the magician of the theatre. Did you ever want to be a magician? I see by your expression you never thought of that.*

a.n. You know what I think, I think all artists have to be magicians. Look, a painter has a canvas, and the first stroke he makes upon the canvas must be a part of the illusionary thing, which is the final thing. I mean, even if you paint realistically, the tree isn't there, you have to give the sense of its presence. This thing isn't there until by your skill and magic you make the thing occupy the space that before did not have it. That is part of the basic definition of art. If the stone is there and I point to it, I'm not an artist, but if I lift the stone and place it elsewhere, the very removal of it, that choice is one of the first steps in the art process. I can't point to the Grand Canyon and then claim that I'd go down in *Who's Who* as the great artist.

e.r. *How long have you been working with your own company?*

a.n. I've had a company, back even in Hartford, as long ago as 1938, '39, but in New York, I think the company, with its present identification, was born around 1951 and 1952. This was about five years after I had started to teach and direct the work at Henry Street Playhouse. I had marvelous young people with me, like Murray Louis, Gladys Bailin, and Phyllis Lamhut. These young people, with their great spirit and vitality and thirst for exploration and also with the great sense of wanting to be challenged, made a unit that was so vital that the company was formed.

e.r. *I understand that you'll soon be leaving New York to go on tour.*

a.n. Yes, this will be quite an extensive tour, my third very extensive tour of Europe and Africa.

e.r. *Do you find it exciting to bring your theatre to various parts of the world?*

a.n. Oh, yes. I love it. I love it. What was very interesting last year was the sequence of historical, architectural theatre that we went through. For example, we opened in Venice at the Finelli, which is that marvelous eighteenth-century theatre; it's not only beautiful, but wonderfully equipped backstage. Then we went to huge theatres like the big opera house in Munich, the National Theatre, which is a restoration of one of their early baroque theatres; and then on into Hamburg, which has a very modern opera house. From there, we traveled to Athens, and actually played in the amphitheatre of Herodes Atticus at the foot of the Acropolis. We then went on to the Baalbeck Festival in Lebanon, where we played in front of the Temple of Bacchus amidst this square mile of ruins.

e.r. *Outside?*

a.n. Yes, and that was the night the astronauts landed on the moon. And here we were, on the steps of this ancient temple with the moon above and my dance going on. These three things all happening at the same time; it was an unforgettable experience. Yes, extraordinary.

e.r. *Since we last spoke, I've read that the French government has invited you to form a national, modern dance company in France. I think it's an exciting project and an enormous compliment to your work. I'd like to know more about it.*

a.n. Whatever one might think of the French or regard as French characteristics, nevertheless, I think the test of fire is in Paris. If one is successful there, it means one becomes eligible for international affairs, particularly, in the arts. I think this has been true so many times, and it continues to be so because when one survives that test in Paris, one has survived one of the most critically alive audiences in the world. My company had a wonderful Paris success when we appeared there in 1968. We were performing at the Théatre de Champs Elysées, which is a gorgeous, historical theatre, and right during the actual performances there would be regular, audible fights going on in the audience. They weren't really physical fights, but discussions about our work. This is the way the French are. They're never without an opinion and they're quick to let you know what you missed. I think that's one of the reasons why France is such an alive country as far as receptivity of the arts is concerned. Anyway, at the end of one particular performance, a bunch of boos started and the antagonism of the responding bravos was carried to such an extraordinary extent that it made us a phenomenal success. Then the young man who was head of the Paris Festival at that time took the whole company out to Maxim's, and we had a typical French love affair where the town is at your feet. It was fabulous. From that time on, Michael Guy has wanted me to come back and establish some kind of program that would get the French modern dance activities under way and on a strong footing. Guy later became the minister of culture under Pompidou, but when Pompidou died, then, of course, he went out. But he left behind the idea that whenever possible, I should come over and establish something there. He particularly impressed this idea upon the superintendent of dance in France, but it was only last year that I was able to start the project. I've been asked to work for three years, and I'm to train a group of French dancers and help them form a national, contemporary, dance company. At first the French thought that the company would include American dancers, or English, or whomever. I said no, I wasn't interested in that type of company. I was interested in applying certain pedagogical principles or theories to a human cultural group so that I could see whether or not such a group had unique characteristics. I hoped that when my aesthetic theories were applied to the dancers, then they would produce dances or choreography that would develop from their own special, creative source, rather than becoming a second, imitative Nikolais company. I gave the first twenty-four students an eight-month training period last year. Then I chose ten out of the twenty-four to make a basic company. The dancers were chosen for their creative potential, and I chose very well. I think if I were to choose them for just a performing unit, I would have chosen other dancers with stronger, technical abilities. But my theory is that if the dancers are creative, they can always develop stronger technique. Technique is the means toward an end, but if you don't know what the end is, then the technique becomes rather useless. So, I've approached the forming of a company from that end rather than from the technical end and it's worked so far. Just a few weeks ago, I had my audition to choose another twenty-four dancers to be trained this next eight months. I'm contracted to be in France for ten weeks of the year, and the rest of the year, I send master teachers to fill in the gaps. This year there'll have to be two teachers; one for the company and one for the new students. It's quite an enterprise.

e.r. *It sounds like it's in the first training stage at the moment.*

a.n. We've passed one training stage. The ones that have had the eight months of training are now going into the performing stage.

e.r. *And when they perform, are they performing their own works that they've choreographed?*

a.n. That they're developing, yes. The first piece will be entirely their own choreography, though I'm more or less masterminding it in a way. The taxpayers want to see the project in actuality and that's to be considered. The city of Angers is the supporting city and it is putting up a quarter of a million dollars and the French national government is putting up another quarter of a million for this dance project. We've already done six lecture-demonstrations in Angers, and they were fabulously successful. Now, we're scheduled to do the first real production in the Théatre Municipal in Angers at the end of November, the beginning of December.

e.r. *I should think it will be difficult to resist your unique influence. Your work is so individual because of the images you create, which, by the way, always overwhelm me. I'm always amazed at the end of a Nikolais evening.*

a.n. What I'm trying to do there is not superimpose my own artistry on them, but rather my aesthetic theories. One contributing factor that prompted the French government to ask me to do this project is that they were aware of the work of two of my dancers. Carolyn Carlson, whom I trained here in New York and who was with the company for several years, now gives solo performances at the Paris Opera House.

e.r. *I've seen her dance.*

a.n. Did you see her in Paris?

e.r. *No, with your company.*

a.n. She's wonderful. Can you imagine a modern dancer giving solo performances in the Metropolitan Opera House here? I can't even get into the New York State Theatre, much less the Metropolitan. And the last two years, Murray [Louis] has also had an enormous success in Paris, and in France generally. The French government had the faith that since I had created two fine artists who are quite different from one another and from me, that I could do the same with a group of French dancers. This is exactly what I hope to do. The work will have some "Nikolais" characteristics, but I think the characteristics will come essentially from my theory that dance is the art of motion. I think that motion designed for choreography should be unique to that choreography and not have any patterns that are applicable to other creative events. This is a quality that I think most modern dance has lost. There's now been such an overlay of ballet and jazz into the professional dance companies that they have little that distinguishes them from ballet companies. I'm still trying to champion the idea of the unique gesture.

e.r. *The unique gesture . . . right, that was originally so central to the idea of modern dance.*

a.n. For this reason though, there might be the same taste to what I do and what the French group might do.

e.r. *Don't you think that emotion comes through motion itself? I don't mean mimetic or pantomimic gesture, but movement in general?*

a.n. Emotion derives from motion or the lack of motion. It is the source of emotion. In other words, emotion is either the result of motion or the lack of it. If you have a desire to do something and you cannot do this thing because of certain tensions or restrictions, then you have the resulting emotions of gladness, sadness, madness, or whatever obvious ones that we know of. However, there are motions that are merely sensations; that is, the idea of a sensitivity and a reaction to the fact that you're in movement. Psychologists haven't yet determined when sensations become emotions. I think emotion is a reaction to sensation, so that if you have the sensation of the fact that you're moving then your reaction to that sensation is therefore emotion. I don't know whether psychologists will agree to this or not, but this is the basis on which I work. For example, it just came up yesterday in rehearsal when I was giving some criticisms to my company. I said, "You're working emotionally rather than motionally. The character should be created from the motional point of view; that's the dancer's job. The actress creates it from the emotional point of view. You have to approach it as a dancer. You will lose a lot of the sensitivity of your movement behaviorism if you take it from the actress's point of view. You must discover your character through the motional progress because that is your art."

An evening with the Alwin Nikolais Dance Theatre is an incredible theatre experience. (above) **Castings** *(Photo: T. Caravaglia)*

(below) **Aviary: A Ceremony for Bird People** *(Photo: R. Rowley)*

e.r. *That's a fascinating distinction. Then the people in the audience read into the movements?*

a.n. It's a mimetic, kinetic thing whether it's the emotive gesture of the actor or simply the motional things. I think, probably, the best thing to do is to compare it to music, the most abstract art. And even highly abstract music, like a Bach fugue, can affect us in a strong, emotional way. But we cannot say what the nature of the emotion is because it is so extraordinarily deep. We have reason to believe that this type of deep, inner feeling is perhaps richer and deeper than our ordinary, surface emotionalisms. This is why back in 1952 I began to do considerable research into the area of emotional reaction and behaviorism.

e.r. *I felt the emotions coming through when I saw* Gallery [1978] *last month up at Jacob's Pillow.*

a.n. Curiously, in my later works, I have gone a little more into literal things. I've proved enough to myself so that I'm liberated from my own theories, and I don't hestitate to do mimetic things or other things that may not be so abstract.

e.r. *I was sitting close to the stage, and the theatre up at the Pillow is small, and I think the closeness to the stage intensifies the dramatic effect. I don't frequent amusement arcades, but I like pin-ball machines so I wander in and out of those game places once in a while and I thought* Gallery *really captured the honky-tonk atmosphere of a shooting gallery in a carnival or a place like that. It was fun in the beginning, but as the piece built, it got scary on a deep level. The masks, the heads, and the gradual change from honky-tonk to macabre affected me. Also, something of yours that I had read before I'd gone up to Jacob's Pillow might have affected my interpretation. That is, I saw an article in which you said that you were fundamentally a mystic. I was fascinated by that statement both personally and by its relation to your work.*

a.n. I think people tend to be afraid of that concept. Though not young people, so much, because they've gone into Buddhism and into Eastern philosophy and so forth. To a great extent, the practice of our Western religion has become somewhat barren, and the soul needs to search out the meanings of the blackness of life. It's utter nonsense if you feel that we know everything about life. It's impossible. There's still so much we don't know and what you don't know is still a mystery, isn't it? If you can't acknowledge that mystery exists then I don't think you have any business being in the arts because the arts tend to expose or to give you a sense of the meaning of what otherwise would be mysterious or undefinable. That is the dimension of life that makes the artist a necessary part of the community. I think it's functional and not "ivory tower," but the United States is just getting into that period of belief, and only for the last twelve years. Here, people will tend to go to dance or such events because it's culturally effete or fashionable to do so. In France and in many other countries, they go because it's a part of their necessary diet of life.

e.r. *When I saw that statement of yours, I reacted strongly because I'm personally fascinated by the subject. Also, in one way or another, I've been in and out of dance for most of my life, and it's always been an answer to some kind of need that I never knew how to verbalize. But I understand the things that you're saying. I was intrigued when I read your statement, but I think it had an immediate effect on my viewing your work. It seemed to color almost everything; for example, in* Grotto, *I could have looked at the contrast between couples who are clothed in the stretch fabric and the one couple who isn't and seen the movements as a play of form. Instead, I suddenly felt that the faceless couples covered in fabric could've been the ghosts of the other. There were layers, mirroring various thoughts and feelings that emerged as I saw the dance.*

a.n. I like to give images that allow the public to make their own associative reaction. I think this is probably one of the things that I'm master of and have been for years. The image by itself is not so important as its being the catalyst into the onlookers for their own reverberations. This to me is very important. If it's spelled out too strongly on the stage, then you're robbed of that privilege. In France, you know, they have a strong tradition of expressionism. One of my students there had a background of that training and in a study that he did, he bared his soul to the height of his aesthetic revelation. In this one instance, what he did was so corny and bad that I said, "I've just got to tell you off. Number one, this place is called CNCD, which means the Center of National Contemporary Dance, and number two, what you're doing is fifty-year-old garbage. It can be good, but this wasn't good." He said, "But I'm baring my soul and you take this away from me." One of the astute students in the group then said, "But Louis, you didn't give us the opportunity to experience our own reaction. You showed us so much that was obvious that you left us nothing to do, and therefore our reception of your work is barren." That in a way, reflects back to the mystical thing which involves leaving some edge in the work. There's got to be some area of mystery. If you spell everything out, then you take away the privilege of the onlooker's own reactions.

e.r. *To more mundane matters. Since you do the painting for the slides and the masks and the visual work, and you also do the music, the choreography, and, in fact, the whole production; does it take you a long time to make a new ballet?*

a.n. I really don't like to do everything. The one trouble working with abstraction is to communicate verbally to other painters or artists or to whomever might contribute to what you're doing what it is you're trying to do. I work intuitively. I work very much by feel and by sketch-pad methods with the dancers. I feel out the process and I don't know what form it's finally going to take. I cannot predict in advance to a composer or to a painter or to a designer of some kind what I want. I only found one painter I could work with. That was George Constant and he was an extraordinarily good colorist, and for some reason or another he was able to relate to what I was doing. In my earlier days I couldn't afford great artists. Now, I've become so accustomed to doing it all that I find the process is much easier for me to keep doing it myself.

e.r. *What's next on your schedule?*

a.n. Next week [mid-September 1979] we leave for our second tour of the Far East. We begin in Taiwan, then go on to Korea, Malaysia, Java, Bali, Singapore, and Manila. I think I skipped a couple of places, but generally we tour all that area. Then we come back to New York and start preparing for the City Center season which begins the day after Christmas. In the meantime, however, I return to France and spend another three weeks there, and that's when I'll present the new company for the first time.

e.r. *And are you working on a new piece as well during all of this?*

a.n. No. I've finished two new pieces that I haven't yet shown in New York. I hope to have a revival of a short piece in addition to the two other new pieces. This depends on whether I can knock that out before the opening. We always have difficulties. For instance, I planned to do some creative work in rehearsal time, but instead I have to put in two new substitutes as two dancers got ill on our South American tour.

e.r. *Your schedule alone, even without problems, sounds enormously demanding.*

a.n. Yes, it is. I try and get six weeks time for a new work, but you never know what's going to happen to interfere with those plans.

e.r. *You must keep going and going and going.*

a.n. Yes, because of all these new tours coming up. We do a West coast tour and then we return to Central and South America for a brief time. Our engagement in Guatemala occurred rather curiously. Last year we were touring in Central America and during a stopover, I picked up an English-language newspaper. When I got on the plane with the dancers, I opened the paper, and on the front page was a picture of a massacre in El Salvador. That's where we were heading and I thought, "What in hell are we going there for?" Fortunately, the plane stopped in Guatemala and the embassy people came and took us off the plane. We were kept in Guatemala for three days and weren't permitted to go on to El Salvador, but I was quite in agreement with that, I must say. While we were in Guatemala, I said we would be happy to do something for them. So we did a class on the stage of the new theatre there which hadn't yet been opened. So now, Guatemala has been included in the next touring schedule of Central and South America.

e.r. *You must have a whole subseries of adventures wherever you go.*

a.n. There's always one somewhere. Every foreign tour we take usually goes through ten or twelve countries, and you can be sure one or two of them are going to be in trouble. So far the trouble has occurred before or after our being there. I hope we never hit one where things are stirring. But I just got a request from all places, Lebanon. It's such a mess now, but I got a request asking if I would write my memories of that night when the astronauts landed on the moon. That was such a fabulous experience. I must confess that when I described it in the last interview we did, I really got very romantic about it.

Alwin Nikolais and Murray Louis share a converted factory loft off Manhattan's Broadway on Eighteenth Street. Like a number of other dance companies who have recently bought factory lofts, the Nikolais-Louis Foundation has stripped the old loft bare and transformed its enormous area into dance studios and offices. Nikolais occupies the top floor of this building, which still has factories and showrooms in operation, but no other dance studios.

I get off the self-service elevator and am buzzed through the main door, past a glass encased cubicle, a remnant of the previous business. Once I pass through the door, I walk into what is obviously the home of an artistic enterprise. International posters, like souvenir picture postcards, decorate the corridors; colorfully painted, makeshift walls mark off the dance-studio space, and the familiar sound of a piano mixes with the sputtering of an electrician's drill. Somewhat early for the scheduled twelve-o'clock interview, I wait in a comfortable room that serves as the office for both companies: the Nikolais Dance Theatre and the Murray Louis Dance Company. Files line one wall and are a reminder that keeping track of the numerous productions and tours adds up to a full-time administrative job. Seeing a company perform is misleading to the extent that it appears to be a self-sufficient, glamorous entity, while what is on display is only the brightest glow of a large structure. As in any performing art, it is the artistic event which is of primary interest; but without the support of an administrative substructure, it would be difficult for the artist's vision to be seen by anyone other than its creator. It takes a wall full of files, a room with five desks, and someone pounding on a typewriter to remind me of the fact that the Nikolais Dance Theatre is a complex, business organization which exists for the sole purpose of expressing the artistic vision of its creator.

In the next moment Alwin Nikolais strides into the office and for an instant I don't recognize him. He has slimmed down so much since the last time I saw him on stage at the Beacon Theatre that not only does he look extremely fit, but he resembles the young dancer at the start of his career I see in my mind's eye. We go off to the quiet of an adjoining room to talk, where cans of film, technical equipment, and notebooks clearly marked with the titles of dance pieces are stored. As he begins to speak of his work and his ideas, Nikolais's eyes sparkle with delight. He is even more effervescent in face-to-face conversation then when taking a curtain call. Meeting Alwin Nikolais again, independent of an evening with the Nikolais Dance Theatre, is totally enjoyable and not in the least confusing. The man himself, apart from his work, is an extremely charming, articulate person who smiles and chuckles with lively enthusiasm while discussing a beguiling mélange of thoughts and experiences.

There is always a certain fascination with an artist whose vision is unique, strong, and personal. This is true of all the arts, not of dance alone. I know I've wondered at times about the life and the person whose perceptions and artistry have affected my own sensibilities through their novels, paintings, or music. Perhaps some of this interest in the artistic creator develops because I, like everyone else, realize that some aspect of the artist's life and personality finds its way into the art product. I wonder how one leads into the other and try to understand the power of artistic expression through the source of its inspiration, the artist.

Alwin Nikolais's work is in the contemporary aesthetic of the individual statement of both form and content. His is an extremely imaginative vision of dance that makes full use of the theatrical experience of illusion to push the audience beyond its habitual responses. Dance in Nikolais's hands is an extension of movement through empathetic play with the human form. In over twenty-five years of developing his ideas and his work, Nikolais has created a long list of theatrical pieces that dazzle the senses by combining surreal images of color, form, and movement. In these Nikolais-created dramas, the original images, masks, and movements extend our sensations and perceptions past our usual, mundane, visual interpretation of the familiar world. Though the works are abstract and do not tell literal, plotted stories, the mood and the images of the piece can be frightening and bleak as Nikolais takes a blunt, realistic look at man's rational and irrational behavior. It is partly this extension into the darker moods and places of the human experience and partly the wizardry of his imagination that have made me so curious about the artist behind the choreography.

But if I happen to wonder about the man who dreams up these visions, then that's just one of my reactions to his work. My focusing on the man instead of the work might be a barrier to keep myself from feeling the work itself. It's usually a futile exercise to separate the artist from the art form. The artist, as the source of the work, is at once deeply connected to his own creations, yet at the same time mysteriously apart. Alwin Nikolais is all the things I feel in his work, and he is also a happy, painstaking craftsman. The enthusiasm and joviality that reaches out to the audience in those after-the-performance curtain calls is the true expression of Nikolais's personality, for it's the work that he does which gives him such a happy countenance.

What makes Alwin Nikolais special, an artist instead of a manipulator of technical apparatus, are his concepts and feelings about the human experience and the artistic talent that enables him to communicate these feelings to other people. An evening spent with the Nikolais Dance Theatre leads into an unknown unwinding of feelings, thoughts, and experiences which is the object of all his creative work. And the evening itself, on another level, may also be a visit with the man himself.

When our interview is over, Nik goes back to rehearsing his company in preparation for the upcoming tour of the Far East. I leave the building, take the subway home, and once there start to transcribe our conversation. Hearing again something that has taken place, but no longer exists in time except in memory and on the piece of tape that I'm hearing, is as eerie as the bone people of Nikolais's *Imago* or the tangled web of *Tensile Involvement*.

A Moment with Bella Lewitzky

There's always the deliciousness of a surprise. . . .

ALL DURING THE SUMMER DANCE SESSION at Connecticut College, there are performances and lectures for the benefit of the students in attendance and other dance enthusiasts who travel to the campus's Palmer Auditorium for events unavailable elsewhere. On one such evening about ten years ago, the theatre was filled to capacity with people who had come to see and hear a lecture-demonstration by a visitor from the West Coast. Bella Lewitzky, a dancer/choreographer whose fame had preceded her across the continent, had actually materialized one summer evening here on the East Coast.

Like all self-contained worlds, the world of dance has its own grapevine along which all sorts of information travels. It was through this vague sort of relay system that I know of Bella Lewitzky's reputation as a brilliant dancer. Even though I had never been to California, never seen Bella dance, never seen her company perform, I know that Lester Horton had worked out his technique on her body because she could do anything. I know that Bella had been co-founder with Lester in establishing the Los Angeles Dance Theatre back in 1946, a time when the arts in the Los Angeles area were practically nonexistent outside of the movie industry. And I know it was Lester Horton and his associates, primarily Bella Lewitzky, who had worked hard to develop dance as an art form in a cultural atmosphere indifferent to their vision. So as I take my seat in this theatre associated with the educational development of East Coast modern dance, I eagerly await Bella Lewitzky, the woman who has never left her own base in California to join a somewhat more supportive environment here in New York, but has remained a staunch pioneer.

The audience understands what it means to pioneer as a dance artist and greets Bella with a standing ovation. As she steps to the podium, I see that she is small and slight, with the kind of compact body that many dancers have. Her dark hair is pulled tightly to the top of her head, revealing a refined, intelligent face. Bella is poised, her voice warm and assured, and she is serious as the talk, now in process, makes clear. "Dancing expresses my feelings in kinetic terms. I keep making discoveries while I dance." Bella's words express an enviable clarity of vision. Continuing the lecture-demonstration, she discusses her approach to technique, to danc-

The taut graciousness of an embodied ideal. Bella Lewitzky (Photo: Tony Esparza)

90

ers, to her work. "Dancing produces a straight hot energy and this is something I can communicate, something I can choreograph." I would like to arrange an interview, but programing problems prevent me from making any contact.

Bella Lewitzky's appearance at Connecticut College is my first encounter with the West Coast modern dance world. To me, as an East Coast person, California is a romantic, legendary area of the United States and is far, extremely far, from New York, where I live. Some of the mythic imagery that exists in my mind is connected to California's natural beauty: the open space, the desert, the mountains, and the Pacific Ocean. Part of the romance comes from the adventure stories of the fabled gold rush. And part from the history of modern dance, for legend has it, that Isadora Duncan envisioned her free, naturalistic dance while running on the beach alongside the pounding Pacific. Ruth St. Denis and Ted Shawn chose California for their first Denishawn School. Martha Graham grew up in California and attended the Denishawn School. Somehow, California became the inspirational, pioneering lodestone for the American modern dance, giving all those who touched it an ongoing deposit of visionary strength.

If heredity can be accepted as an influence on a person's life, then it would be easy to understand how Bella Lewitzky emerged as a pioneering dancer/choreographer, for her parents immigrated from Russia to join a utopian community in the Mojave desert. As the daughter of an idealistic, pioneering family, Bella grew up in an intellectually elevated atmosphere, nurtured not only by philosophical concepts, but by the stillness and beauty of the surrounding desert and mountains. As a child, Bella loved to move, but she was not introduced to formal dance training until she reached high school. When she was seventeen, a ballet teacher's partner told her of Lester Horton's work, and she enrolled as his student.

Bella immediately felt at home in Lester's classes and knew that her feelings about dance were closer to Lester's work than to any other form of dance she had seen. She joined his school and remained with him, working closely with him both as a dancer and associate until 1950, when she left to begin work on her own.

In 1951, Bella founded her own Dance Associates, an organization that echoed the original Dance Theatre by combining a school, theatre, and performing group. Her present organization, the Bella Lewitzky Dance Company, was formed in 1966. Since then the company has traveled internationally, receiving exciting reviews that praise the lightness, airiness, and optimism of her choreography. The European reviewers, especially, speak of the feeling of space, sun, and openness that exist in her work, and which, they find, reflect their own images of California.

Bella's involvement with dance extends into the field of dance education; she has been the Dean of the School of Dance at the California

Institute of the Arts and dance chairperson of the Idlewild Arts Foundation
at the University of Southern California. She has also been a member of
UNESCO's International Dance Association, and holds, among her many
citations and prizes, the annual Dance Magazine Award, a Guggenheim
Foundation Fellowship, and a grant from the Mellon Foundation.

Recently I had an unexpected opportunity to visit Los Angeles—
actually to see this mythic place. My stay there was too short for me to
absorb the full California experience, but I did feel the vast expanse of
space, and I did schedule that meeting with Bella Lewitzky. Her dance
company was on vacation, so I was unable to see either the classes at her
school or any performances of her work. Ironically, the company was on
its way to an engagement in New York City.

In the meantime, I met Lewitzky herself, and my original impression
was reinforced by her candid friendliness and her ideas, as refreshing as a
cactus flower in the midst of a colorless desert. Her very being radiates the
taut graciousness of an embodied ideal. Speaking to her, I am aware that a
lifetime of dedicated experience deepens the meaning of her words, and I
am reminded of that extraordinary period of time when I was first exposed
to modern dance. It was a time of overflowing dedication and the intense
spirit pervaded everything it touched: performances, choreographers,
dancers, teachers, students. Now, meeting Bella Lewitzky, I again experience that dedicated vision, integrity, intelligence, and love of the dance
that made the pioneering period of American modern dance so fiercely
precious.

e.r. *Was there anything left of the original Denishawn School when you
began studying modern dance here in Los Angeles?*

b.l. I really knew no vestige of it. As a matter of fact, it had disappeared
so totally that it was only in later years that I found out the Denishawn School had been initiated here.

e.r. *I was curious about that. I would have thought there were some
fragments left.*

b.l. Apparently all its practitioners left to reestablish a Denishawn school
in the East, and that's probably why it disappeared and left no trace.

e.r. *Lester Horton, the man you studied with, came from the Midwest, I
believe.*

b.l. Yes, from Indiana. Lester's background is rather interesting. He had
little formal dance training, a fair amount of theatre training, but he
wanted to work in the theatre. Somewhere in his schooling, he fell in
love with the American Indian and began to stage pageants, of which
one was *Hiawatha*. He organized masses of people on a riverbank
somewhere in Indiana and a wealthy woman, who either came originally from California or wanted to come out here, saw the pageant
and was interested in repeating that type of pageant here in Califor-

nia, so she brought Lester out and was his first sponsor. And that's
how he happened to come out to California.

e.r. *From general information about Lester Horton, it seems that a lot of*
the technique he worked with was originally based on improvisational
studies.

b.l. There was a great deal of it—we did a lot of exploratory things.

e.r. *Now classes are given in Horton technique. It looks very fluid, very*
open. When you were working with Lester, did you realize that you
were developing a "Horton technique"?

b.l. I don't think we particularly thought in terms of labels. When we
began formulating what is now called the Horton technique there was
something known as the Graham technique, the Humphrey-Weidman
technique, the Wigman technique. We had heard more than we had
seen of these, because coast-to-coast communication was very distant. We simply, from what we had read, decided that we didn't want
to fall into the school of "isms," but rather establish as our objective
a body of training that would make for maximum range of motion, as
devoid as possible of style and therefore usable for a choreographer in
all directions. That is what we set out to do, though it was strongly
influenced by Lester's artistic eye selecting the kind of thing he fa-
vored. Its direction was exploratory at first, and then he began to
codify some of the work. But it would have changed year to year. All
techniques change year to year as long as the creator is still alive
because the creator will be creating. These things freeze and become
rigid doctrines after the creator is no longer alive. That's one reason
why I've never taught Horton technique. Second is that I don't think
that I could remember it because I've gradually moved into my own
materials. I no longer distinguish between where his materials end
and mine take over. If I can recall a straight piece of Horton technique, I'll identify it as such, but what people are teaching as Horton
technique, I haven't a clue, although it was fashioned on my body.

e.r. *I've only glimpsed it at the Ailey school. The class was coming across*
the floor and it seemed to me there was an openness to the
movements.

b.l. There is. I recall that, too.

e.r. *Was Horton the focal point of any modern dance in L.A. during the*
1940's?

b.l. He was one of the primary figures. There were others. Virginia Hall
Johnson, who I think was Graham in her base, and there were some
people, like Eleanor King, who just moved on their own. And Miss
Ruth worked out here in those years.

e.r. *I once attended a lecture-demonstration at Connecticut College*
Summer Dance Session at which you spoke. I remember that you said
that you didn't accept virtuosity as an end; that that wasn't what you

thought dance was about nor what it meant to you. You may have to correct my memory.

b.l. I still feel that way. I think when virtuosity becomes an end in itself, that the art form is in a strong decline. It's a dangerous symptom of a degenerating art form.

e.r. *You mean when there's neither motivation nor connection between the acrobatics and the theme?*

b.l. Virtuosity should serve a purpose which really subsumes the technique. The technique in and of itself is a tool. It should not, in my mind, be the dance form. The dance form should be what you are trying to say with technique. Even if it's merely a "dancey" dance, there still is quality, there's perception, there's some kind of vision and no matter how nonliteral or how abstract, there is something you are saying. But when you are on exhibit as an Olympian athlete then that's virtuosity as an end in itself. I favor technical skills, but I favor them the way an opera star or a violinist or a Pablo Casals has a technique at his command which is certainly virtuosic, but that's not the function of it. It's so that he or she can use this great range of dexterity to render the composition more exquisite. The composition is what is there. That's the form. I still feel that way, so I apparently have made little change since you heard me.

e.r. *Then you usually have some particular idea when you start to choreograph a dance?*

b.l. I hardly ever choreograph a piece only to use it as a vehicle of display. I don't think I've done one, well, maybe I have, but I don't think I have.

e.r. *I have the impression of plasticity in the work of your dancers, and that requires a lot of strength and skill.*

b.l. I train as vigorously as anyone trains. My dancers are good jumpers; they have high extensions, and they are strong. I have a particular objective in that I hope that flexibility and strength are absolutely evenly weighed in their development. I do *train* to virtuosity, but I don't *serve* virtuosity.

e.r. *I understand the distinction.*

b.l. That's my objective, whether I achieve it or not, I don't know. Only time can tell that; I cannot.

e.r. *Do the dancers who work with you come with other training?*

b.l. Sometimes. If they begin with minimal training, then they are basically trained by me, but it's also true that I take dancers trained from other areas and then they are retrained and adapt to both the repertory and the outlook suitable for this company.

e.r. *How many dancers are in your company?*

b.l. Ten. It's just right.

e.r. *That's a nice size.*

b.l.   I like to be in touch with all aspects, so this size works for me.

e.r.   *Do you work closely with the musicians and artists who work on your dances?*

b.l.   I've been very fortunate. I worked for the first several years with a woman named Cara Bradbury-Rhodes-Marcus. Many of my ballets were composed by her. We shared in the creative process—that is, when I began a work, she would come in and clock it, watch it, absorb it, and begin to live in it. Then she would come back with some ideas that were musical parallels, and we would discuss them, share them, and that gave the work a single viewpoint. I've also worked with one light designer, Darlene Neel, and again, she is a strong, artistic contributor. She also has done the majority of my wardrobe and so it comes from one force, one generic line. You see no conflicting overlays or contrary viewpoints, and I treasure that. I like that unity of intent and recently I've been fortunate to collaborate with Rudi Gernreich [fashion designer]. We grew up together in the same dance world, so we also share the same kind of concept.

e.r.   *In that way, the dance remains a whole.*

b.l.   Yes, there's a kind of integrity that ensues. I'm now working with my present musical director, Larry Attaway, who just did two beautiful scores for me. And we work in the same way. He is so close to the material that he's my best coach. I can turn a ballet over to him and he'll bring it back to its original intent, which is a great trait. It requires a certain kind of eye, a certain kind of insight and a fine memory. I've been extremely lucky.

e.r.   *Do you notate or record your dances?*

b.l.   I used to notate in my own form of shorthand and then three years later, I would pick up my notes and they might as well have been written in Sanskrit. I hadn't a clue about what I originally meant. These personal languages sound clear at the moment, but the notes can only kick off what I already know. Therefore, by the time that I return to the original notes, I've moved away from that work to another and I no longer remember what I meant. I've found that my method is of very little value. Then we went to 8mm film, but there wasn't any sound at that point, and it had that weakness. We couldn't always put it together with sound. Then we went to Super 8, which had sound, and that was a step upwards. Recently, we've gone to video which has the advantage of playback and it can be wiped clean and so on. We record our dances on videotape now, and that too, is very weak because, as you know, one of the human elements is error. So something done incorrectly gets recorded for all posterity and for a

"The dance form should be what you are trying to say with technique." Bella Lewitzky Dance Company in **Inscape** *(Photo: Dan Esgro)*

new dancer. There's no way to avoid that. And a dancer has to look over backward when learning a role. We've always threatened to put up a mirror image, which I'm sure would solve that problem, but we've never had the luxury of time or money to arrange that.

e.r.   I've never thought of that. Don't you videotape when it's all finished?

b.l.   Oh, yes. It's the process of learning the role I'm referring to. But a work is never all finished. I'll come in two years later and say "Why did I do that?" I'll fix a section or a new dancer will replace an old dancer and the new person will, quite appropriately, put on the role like a suit of clothing that fits *them*, and not the originator of the role. If it doesn't distort the original intent, then it's logical that the new dancer should find whatever is correct and good for that person's physiognomy and psyche. Indeed, that's part of the creative act of the performer. But many a role will slip via my changes or via the changes made by alternating people; and the danger comes with the third person. The original intent might have shifted critically by then, and then one indeed must go back. That's when the original videotape is of great value. I can see what the originator of the role did and what the intent was, even though it has since been changed a little here or there. We must then return it to its original form.

e.r.   Then it's a guide. What you're saying now about a role changing reminds me of a quote of yours that I read and admired. "Art is in an ongoing process and the only constant is change . . ."

b.l.   I think I'm a stick-in-the-mud. I still feel that. I do. I think what we were describing about the process of making a dance itself is to all intents and purposes something that is fixed. That is, the dance is a set object like a book or a piece of music. But in the field of dance, a dance work keeps changing as long as it is alive. I guess it is that presence, the *nowness* of it that makes the process of change possible. I think I love dance and find it so fascinating because it is in process all of the time.

It is also true that the form itself evolves and is in process. If I were to define modern dance, for example, I would have to say modern dance 1918 or modern dance 1950 and so on. Anyhow, modern dance is a catch-all phrase that only distinguishes certain things about it and they're usually negative things. That it's not a form of dance confined to the five positions, does not work on pointe, is not entertainment dance as commercial dance is. Those things remain constant, but the use of the form itself, the art, is in process all of the time. That is one of my greatest love affairs in the practice of the art of dance.

e.r.   The possibility of growth?

b.l.   It's never the same tomorrow as it is today, which is different than yesterday.

e.r.   That's like nature as well.

b.l. But I think that's true. I think when you speak of things that move and I don't mean to turn deeply philosophic, but when you use the word "move," you are speaking of change. Motion is another description of change, in the main. And dance is a motion art form. Perhaps the process of change is always more present with the dance. I, anyhow, react to it and like it. For me it's all of the secret places where the pleasure lies.

e.r. *It's like constantly touching the unknown.*

b.l. Exactly. You can have educated guesses, but there's always the deliciousness of a surprise. "Oh, I didn't know that was going to happen. Oh, look, didn't that go in that direction? I didn't know it was going to . . ." But the choreographic process, I think, for all choreographers, must certainly contain that element. You think you know where you're headed with day one, but by day three, it's already exhibited something that isn't precisely what you thought it was and it is surprising. Sometimes in a very alarming fashion, and sometimes in a very pleasing fashion, but I can never just sit down, encircled by formulas, and play. It doesn't work for me.

e.r. *Part of choreographing is this process that you describe?*

b.l. Dance is not a fixed thing. It's not a painting on a wall, which would be far more saleable in this day. I've often wanted to frame a dance and see if it too would bring in the rewards that paintings do today, but it isn't like a painting on a wall. It doesn't grow in the eyes of the observer, it grows in the arms of the performer. It's different. Dance comes alive in the process of the performance; primarily, through the creativity of the performer. It's an interesting difference, I think.

e.r. *It's an interesting interaction between the dance itself and the performing of it. You've not only been active in creating and teaching dance in your own school, but you've been involved with school programs, advisory panels for the government, and arts programs; in fact the whole development of dance during the last decade.*

b.l. I feel the dance field has given me such an abundance of experience, pleasure, insight, and information. And I have very little interest in taking all of that with me to the grave. I would like to feed it back again in as many ways as I can. I inherited a great deal in my apprenticeship with Lester, and also I gained much from the artists around him and the time in which I grew, which was a very special time because it was the birthing period, or close to the birthing period, of modern dance. I form a link with that past, and I think the only immortality that I believe in is that kind of a cultural inheritance. I'm involved in passing it on and serving as a link to the people with whom I come in touch. If I can in any way be a spokesperson or a conduit to aid in the continuity and healthy vitality of dance, then I'm interested in that. I tend to be an ardent and optimistic joiner. I always believe something wonderful will happen ''If only . . .'' The organizations all sound wonderful and full of what is needed to have happen. Sometimes I permit myself to belong to more things than I have any right to belong to. Then I say I must not, and pull back because I cannot do anything adequately if I spread myself so thin. I'm at that point now.

e.r. *Do you find when you speak about dance that people today under-stand more about the subject?*

b.l. I don't know. I think rather than a difference in understanding, I think there's a difference in size. When I began, the people who were around modern dance were passionate advocates. They were disci-ples of a new art form. They were passionate, devoted, fanatical, prejudiced, intolerant, and all those exciting things. But they were only a handful. I mean they were like three or four people, which, of course, is a gross exaggeration, but not in terms of the entire populace.

e.r. *I'm familiar with some of that.*

b.l. This small following of devotees knew intimately about the art form. They were well informed, but if you spoke to people outside this narrow circle, they would not know what you meant if you said dance. Then if you said modern dance, that was baffling beyond belief. Today I find that that circle of people who are devoted, is far, far wider, and less penetrating in the main. I don't think the knowledge is better, I think it's broader.

e.r. *That's an interesting distinction.*

b.l. I'm not sure I'm right. There is a much broader awareness of all of the dance forms.

e.r. *Without the intensity?*

b.l. Without the intensity, but I think that's because there is so much more. The field itself is not as intense. There's a lot, and there's a lot of variety. There's a lot of variety in the audience, as well.

e.r. *Your company has an active touring schedule.*

b.l. Yes. We're a touring company. That's how we earn our living. That's how we support ourselves. Not in very magnificent style, but it af-fords the dancers the opportunity to dance without also waiting on tables, as many dancers must still do. So, they've learned to travel like gypsies.

e.r. *Your love of dance goes very deep. You've said, in fact, "There is a love and regard and belief in dance."*

b.l. The art of dance has been a way that I've maintained growth. It has made me grow and it has helped me to grow. And yes, I guess I'm very much in love with it. The word dance creeps in because that is my art, but I think that all arts are a way the individual can make realizable the world in which they live.

If we looked at the body of knowledge that exists outside ourselves, it would be so mind-boggling that we would blow fuses. There is no way we can comprehend all the things that are actually visible to us. Some of it is too large to be borne, actually, too large to cope with. If you view it through the objectifying element of the arts, it renders both the unknown and the known into possible symbology which stems from you to that unknown, to that outside, to that environment in which you find yourself. You can shape portions of it in a measurable way. Now you can deal with it because it has shape, it has form.

I think of the arts as shaping and forming and symbol-making. The arts make an infinity workable. If you cannot make that experience into shapes you can handle, that you can perceive, that you can guess about, that you can attempt to define and objectify, it is impossible to cope. So the arts for me, and for, I think, almost all people, brings this kind of clarity and coping to much of our life. I guess that is another way of saying what I think learning is. I really do feel that. One of the reasons that I became an advocate of arts in the schools is because I feel that all children should have the option to be symbol-makers, to be formers, to be able to objectify their perceptions and their conceptions, even when they're quite young.

An Introduction to Alvin Ailey

One needs dancers to make dances, so I made a company.

P*EOPLE can somehow identify with the things we're going through on the stage. It's a human thing, the emotions.*

An individual's statement, but one that reflects the common feelings of four dancers from the Alvin Ailey American Dance Theatre to whom I am chatting during a break in their rehearsal time. The dancers are in the midst of preparing for the upcoming season at New York's City Center Theatre, but they know from past experiences that their long hours of constant rehearsals will be rewarded by overwhelming audience support. For people everywhere respond with enthusiastic applause and cheers to the contagious excitement of their dancing.

It's the same human thing. When I saw this company, I was involved with what was happening on stage, and for weeks afterwards, I was excited by it.

The dancers are Kelvin Rotardier, Consuela Atlas, Linda Kent, and Dudley Williams. All feel that the strong Ailey repertoire and the way the company moves influenced each one's own desire to become a dancer in the company. Though they share this common bond and now, in a sense, belong to the same family, their backgrounds are surprisingly different: Kenneth comes from Trinidad, Consuela from Boston, Linda is one of the few white dancers in this predominantly black company, and Dudley has been a dancer with Martha Graham's company.

We don't dance mechanically, we're not fictitious. We relate on a very human level, I think. It's kind of communicating love, joy: that's what always impressed me about the company when I first saw them back in '63. There was a joy to it.

Though the choreographer's ideas, insights, movements, patterns, and musicality create the material for a dancer to use, the ultimate factor in bringing any dance to life is the dancer's dancing. Thus, the dancers be-

A large, direct-speaking man full of positive energy. Alvin Ailey (Courtesy of the Alvin Ailey Dance Company)

come the choreographer's instrument for communicating his or her ideas to the audience. When the dancers believe in the choreographer's vision and are in harmony with the work, their commitment gets relayed to the audience.

I do think the people who come to see us get the feeling it could be them we're talking about, or dancing about. Or it could be someone they know, and they get to understand themselves more.

The choreographer is responsible for the special look and excitement of the company, since his job includes choosing the dancers and creating dance roles for or "on" them. Physicality, i.e., size, proportions, color, and quality of movement define each dancer and so are factors considered by a choreographer in choosing a dancer to realize an imagined role. When three-quarters of the dancers in the Alvin Ailey American Dance Theatre are black, and half the repertory they dance is rooted in the black experience, then this experience becomes an essential aspect of what the choreographer wishes to communicate to the audience.

I've heard people say they hate us too, but they come to see us; but, that's human. To be human is to be loved and to be hated.

Ailey's own choreography for his company divides into two primary categories of equal importance. One is related to the black experience and includes works such as *Revelations, Mary Lou's Mass, Blues Suite.* These ballets are based on the music of spirituals, blues, contemporary popular music, and are the pieces that are typically associated with Ailey and his company. The second basic category is composed of abstract ballets like *Streams* and *Lark Ascending.* These are choreographed to classical music (Igor Stravinsky, Vaughan Williams, etc.) and fuse a modern and balletic dance vocabulary. Related to the first category, but more personal, are the solo pieces *Reflections in D, Cry, Hermit Songs;* and there is also another subcategory in which the dramatic characterizations (*Flowers, Masekela Language*) spill directly out of the black experience into contemporary social problems.

Most of the guest choreographers who work with the Alvin Ailey American Dance Theatre are black, and they explore the same American black experience, but from their individual points of view. Sometimes, Ailey invites young choreographers outside of the black experience to work with the company. Most recently, he has also started a heritage movement to revive early key works in the history of American modern dance. These include pieces by seminal choreographers, black and white, like Katherine Dunham, Pearl Primus, Ted Shawn, Lester Horton, and Jack Cole.

His [Alvin Ailey's] source of inspiration is the black heritage, but basically he's involved in a beautiful thing happening on stage; whether it's black or white is unimportant.

The uniqueness of the Alvin Ailey American Dance Theatre, however, comes from the evocation of deeply embedded experiences that are special to the American black heritage. Through the choice of music, through stylized gestures, and through the story lines, which are often sung, the company's choreographers, Alvin Ailey, Talley Beatty, Donald McKayle, and George Faison, use this particular background as a base; from this base they transform the emotional essence of their experiences into the universally shared feelings of love, hate, fear, and exultation. And the dancers, a group of fast-moving, outstanding performers, brazenly deliver their message to the world.

Alvin just draws from what he knows, from his childhood, and how can you do a dance about something you don't know?

Yes, Alvin Ailey filters his own knowledge of the American black experience through loving eyes. In the process he has created a popular dance-theatre company that reaches far beyond rhetoric to communicate an emotional truth about an important, often misunderstood, cultural experience. I have learned from this work, and I appreciate his passion. Yet, on my way to the upcoming interview, I choose not to discuss his very obvious role as a leading black choreographer. Instead, I decide to look at the man behind the Alvin Ailey American Dance Theatre in the same way his dancers do, as a man who loves to make beautiful movement, beautiful dancing. So, when I meet Alvin Ailey, a large, direct-speaking man full of positive energy, I avoid the obvious. And we talk of this and that.

e.r. *Mr. Ailey, when did you form the Alvin Ailey American Dance Theatre?*
a.a. The company first came into being in 1958, although it has changed personnel. It's grown from one performance in 1958 to two in 1959, and so on and on and on until 1971.
e.r. *How many dancers are in your company now? [1971]*
a.a. There are sixteen dancers in the company. We started with eight and we've grown steadily over the years. We just came back from a very successful tour of the Soviet Union and they were rather amazed that we could do so many things with so few people, because every small company over there has at least sixty dancers.
e.r. *Back in 1958, what prompted you to form your own company?*
a.a. Well, I had been a dancer, and as a matter of fact, when I formed the company I was dancing with it; but I stopped dancing in 1965. I guess I made the company as a medium for myself to choreograph. I wanted to make dances, and like a painter giving a show, or a sculptor sculpt-

ing, one needs dancers to make dances, so I made a company for that reason.

e.r. *From a very practical point of view.*

a.a. Right.

e.r. *Are you making any new dances now?*

a.a. We're going to present about ten ballets from a repertoire of twenty-five, and I'm making two new pieces in three weeks. It's rather hectic. We're going to do the first one on the first night. It's titled *Archipelago*, and I've choreographed it to a piece of music by a Bulgarian composer by the name of Boucourechliev. The full company dances in it, and in the second week of the season we're having a guest artist from the Royal English Ballet, Lynn Seymour, who is one of their principal dancers.

e.r. *Are both of these ballets yours?*

a.a. Yes. The piece I'm doing for Lynn Seymour is called *Flowers*, and that is sort of about contemporary female rock singers.

e.r. *Is Lynn Seymour going to do it on pointe?*

a.a. Half on pointe and half off. It starts off pointe and then goes on pointe.

e.r. *A little like your ballet,* The River?

a.a. Something like *The River*.

e.r. *Will your company be doing* The River *as well?*

a.a. No, I don't think so. It isn't even finished yet. At the moment it belongs to Ballet Theatre. Actually, the work belongs to the choreographer, but I think it's Ballet Theatre's for a while. I'm supposed to finish it next spring, and we shall see.

e.r. *Back to the formation of your company. What made you decide to have a mixed repertoire of ballets by different choreographers? Most of the modern dance groups do not function in that way.*

a.a. They do their own things. I've always believed in mixing. I suddenly started doing it in 1964, after I had been in New York for many seasons and had seen a lot of concerts at the YMHA [Young Men's Hebrew Association], and at Henry Street, and all the dance places. I had seen marvelous works that lasted one performance and then were never seen again. And so I decided if I ever had a company that was functioning, that I would try to rekindle some of these works, and I have done that. And I've gone especially after the works of black choreographers, Talley Beatty, Donald McKayle, Louis Johnson, Geoffrey Holder, and my own fellows who choreograph too. I encourage the boys in my own company to make dances.

e.r. *I think the variety makes your company stimulating.*

a.a. It does. It's very interesting to see a lot of choreographic points of view and a lot of musical points of view in one evening. I think there are probably only two or three people in the whole world who can sustain a whole evening. Maybe only two. I won't name them, but they're both in New York City.

e.r. *That's delicate. When you do a work, do you usually start from the music or an idea?*

a.a. From both. But I do really get a great deal from music. It's partly the music and partly the idea, but if it were weighted on one side, I would say it was the music, yes.

e.r. *I understand the trip to Russia was an enormous success.*

a.a. We left here on September 21st and we got to Russia on September 24th, and we stayed there for six weeks. We played in six different cities, a week for each.

e.r. *Did you cover the whole country?*

a.a. Not the whole country; Russia is enormous you know. We were in the Ukraine for four weeks out of the six, in three tiny little towns that no performer hardly ever went to. The reception in those towns was a little strange; they didn't quite know what to think. They hadn't seen anything like this before, and then in Kiev, that's a major cultural center in the Ukraine, we were very well received. But in Moscow and in Leningrad, the reception was absolutely fantastic. We got a twenty-minute ovation on opening night in Moscow. And the same thing in Leningrad. Then we went on to Paris. We had a season in Paris; a three-day season, if that can be called a season, and then a very successful two-week season at the Sadlers Wells in London where we had them dancing in the aisles. Our key signature piece is *Revelations* and it's danced to spirituals. In London we used an English chorus, but with Brother John Sellers, a black folk singer from here, to do the singing, and the effect was tremendous.

e.r. *You've done a lot of traveling to some very far-away places, like Australia.*

a.a. Yes, we've been to Australia twice. The first time we went, we were on tour for the State Department. We went to Australia and all over Southeast Asia. We've been to Europe five times. We went to the Dakar Festival in Africa in 1966, and we toured East and West Africa in 1966–1967. This past summer, we went to North Africa for five weeks on a State Department Tour that took us to Algeria, Tunisia, and Morocco.

e.r. *How do you find audience response? Does it change in different parts of the world?*

a.a. Yes. It's different in different parts of the world, except a lot of our material is based on black folk heritage. We have a lot of blues, spirituals, and jazz in our repertoire; and we have a lot of Duke Ellington, Miles Davis, Dizzy Gillespie and contemporary music as well as the jazz. The audience always responds favorably to the black music and the black dances.

e.r. *Even when the material is not familiar?*

a.a. Yes. It has a kind of universal appeal. And the feeling of the folk music is the same all over the world. Every culture has spirituals; every culture seems to have blues, and people respond very strongly to that in our work.

1979

e.r. *When we last spoke, in 1971, you had just come back from a trip to Russia. Is the Alvin Ailey American Dance Theatre still doing a lot of world traveling?*

a.a. A tremendous amount of traveling. In the fall of 1979, we'll be touring Europe again. We leave in August, and we'll be in Greece, Hungary, Romania, Poland, France. The company will perform in twelve countries before our return in October.

e.r. *Are these State Department tours?*

a.a. They have a lack of funding, so the State Department now wants you to get yourself over and back. They'll pay for transportation in-between, and arrange certain things, but you've got to set up your own tour.

e.r. *Has the company been traveling like this every year?*

a.a. The company has never stopped traveling. Here in the States, we do a yearly East and West coast tour. We usually go straight across the country, and to part of the South, as well.

e.r. *You must find that audiences everywhere continue to be receptive to your work.*

a.a. Our music is accessible, and so are our themes.

e.r. *In the last few years, you seem to be doing less of your own choreography. Is this because of your role as artistic director of the company?*

a.a. There's a lot going on, and it takes time to choreograph. However, I just did a solo to the music of Charlie Mingus for this last spring season. I also revived two of my earlier works, *Flowers* and *Myth*; and then, I constantly get requests from all over the world to stage my works. I get so many that I can't fulfill all, but I do what I can. The company, and now there are two junior ones in addition to the main one, does take time. Our school has mushroomed unbelievably; we've several thousand students.

e.r. *What are the other two companies?*

a.a. There's the repertory ensemble, a small company that travels all over the smaller cities on the East Coast, and there's the workshop for

"Our key signature piece is **Revelations** *. . . danced to spirituals." Company of the Alvin Ailey American Dance Theatre (Photo: Bill Hilton)*

e.r. *I'm curious about the requests that you receive from other countries.*

a.a. I've set *The River* on the Caracas Ballet in Venezuela and on the Budapest Opera Ballet. I've just done a new work for the Bat Dor Company in Israel that's called *Shigaon*. And of course, here in New York, I've given the Joffrey Ballet *The Mingus Dances* and *Feast of Ashes*. At one point, I even gave *Revelations* to the Ballet Folklorico in Mexico, but only for the Olympics.

e.r. *Do you see a lot of the work of other people in order to choose your own guest choreographers?*

a.a. Yes. Though some of the people I know from years ago. Donald McKayle and I had been talking for a long time about doing *District Storyville*, which we just did, and then George Faison was in my company during the late 60's.

e.r. *I don't know much about your personal background. Where do you come from and how did you get started in dance?*

a.a. I was born in Texas, near Houston, and my mother took me to Los Angeles when I was very young. I became involved in dance when Carmen De Lavallade, who was in one of my classes at school, convinced me to go to Lester Horton. I started out majoring in Romance languages, but my work with Lester eventually took over.

e.r. *You hadn't danced before you studied with Lester?*

a.a. No, just some high school athletics. My mother was interested in my learning music, but in Los Angeles at that time, in the 1940's, there really wasn't much but the movie world. Not much theatre, and no dance performances to speak of, except for the work Lester was doing. A lot of exciting people were around Lester then. Jimmy Truite was there, Bella Lewitzky, and Rudi Gernreich, to name a few. It was a stimulating atmosphere. Lester had us study sculpture and other arts as well as dance. It was a total theatre experience. I worked with clay, with materials, built props, made costumes. Lester thought it was important to work with texture so we developed a strong, tactile sense of theatre materials. There was also a sense of social problems in the group's work and in its thinking even though Lester was doing night-club work to survive.

e.r. *When did you come East?*

a.a. The Horton Company came to the Ninety-Second Street YMHA in '54 to do a concert and of course I was with them. Then, Carmen and I came back to New York and did the Broadway show, *House of Flowers*. After Lester died, we tried to keep the school going, but it was hard. I came back again to New York and did the show *Jamaica*. Arthur Mitchell was the lead dancer in that, and he introduced me to ballet, and to Karel Schook, who later worked with Arthur in developing the Dance Theatre of Harlem. Of course, living in New York, I saw a lot of very good dance and that all had its influence.

e.r. *Are you planning any new works now?*

a.a. I'm always planning.

e.r. *What would you say was the major influence on your own work?*

a.a. The black experience, very definitely. Then, growing up in Los Angeles. For example, *Flowers* isn't just about Janis Joplin. It's about Judy Garland, Marilyn Monroe, or anyone who lived on beauty, became an idol or a movie star, and then couldn't handle it. I've danced in the movies, worked in Hollywood, and I've seen the Hollywood dream factory up close.

e.r. *Other factors?*

a.a. I always spend a great deal of time listening to records, considering them, and working with them.

e.r. *Do you audition your dancers yourself? Must they come from your school?*

a.a. My dancers come from the school, from open calls, and from all over the country. We're always looking when we're on tour.

e.r. *You've a fantastic company of dancers.*

a.a. I think so, too. I look for individuality, not for a particular physical type. And I look for potential, which is why someone doesn't have to be in the other two companies to get into the major one. I particularly need dancers with personalities, because our work is dramatic, and the dancers have to act, have to be comedians. Technique is getting more and more important. The original company couldn't have done *Streams* or *Choral Dances*. Recently, one of my first dancers said, "We couldn't have got into those leotards, never mind cope with the technical challenges," and they were a great company. Dancers today are more highly trained, more technical.

e.r. *When you start a new work, do you usually choreograph with a certain person in mind, or do you find the person after you've done the work?*

a.a. Some of this and some of that. I usually start by working it out on myself and on my assistant. Obviously *Cry* was done for Judy [Jamison].

e.r. *You were the 1979 Capezio Award winner . . .*

a.a. Winning an award is always wonderful, but being recognized makes you have a good look at yourself. You evaluate yourself and what you're doing. The Capezio award is a big award in the dance world, and it made me think, "What have I done," "Where am I?"

e.r. *It seems to me that what you do is very special.*

a.a. It's a question of staying with it, staying on top of all that has to be done.

Alvin's work is all about moving your body. So as a dancer, the color of your skin doesn't make much difference.

The physical look of the Alvin Ailey American Dance Theatre remains predominantly black. The attitude among the dancers in the company towards their individual color differences is the same as it was eight years ago. They say it doesn't make any difference if you can do the work; and they mean it.

In the eye of the public, we're considered predominantly a black company because the pieces which are the most known, Revelations, Blues Suite, *etc. are the pieces that come out of the black experience. But we're multiracial and that's Alvin's specific attempt to make our work more universal.*

Maxine Shulman, Serita Allen, and Peter Woodin are three of the current generation of Ailey dancers. They came to New York from homes in Washington, Arizona, and Pennsylvania and through scholarships and auditions made their way into the company. Teenagers when the Ailey company was establishing its voice in the dance world, they grew up at a time when the developing interest in dance was broadening the base of audience support.

Alvin looks for dancers who will bring some special quality and who can make a strong statement on stage. He really is quick to see if somebody's personality is the kind of personality that will give, and also be versatile enough to do all the things that are expected.

We're all different, but Alvin has a good eye for how we'll look together. Not only does Alvin pick the dancers, but in a way, the dancers pick him. If you were meant to be a part of this company, you get here.

One of the striking parallels between the group of dancers that I'm now talking with and the earlier group is the similarity of their feelings about the human aspect of the Ailey repertoire. The 1979 dancers are just as firmly convinced as the group of Ailey dancers that I had spoken to eight years ago that the range of easily identified human emotions expressed in their work creates an accessible, empathetic bridge between their dancing and the audience. They feel strongly that the audience recognizes its own experiences in their dancing, and this accounts for the overwhelmingly enthusiastic response to their performances. Another ongoing factor is the established pattern of rehearsals, performances, and traveling that operates like a heartless machine usurping all their time and energy. As dancers in a busy company, they have little time to be anything but dancers who dance.

The choreographer basically does the steps and furnishes the concept of the whole work. If Alvin is choreographing, then, of course, he's making the dance right there. He comes in with an idea of what he's trying to do and he knows exactly what the music is doing.

Over the last eight years the Alvin Ailey American Dance Theatre has grown in popularity, achieving what few modern dance companies realize, two regular New York seasons each year. In fact, the company celebrated its twentieth anniversary season in the fall of 1978. With the regular seasons, though, comes the semiannual box office pressure to offer a large repertoire and the excitement of new premieres to audiences who buy the tickets and who, as a group, thrive on variety and glamour.

Alvin doesn't usually come in and give a whole long phrase of movement. He'll give a phrase and see how that looks, then he'll give another, and see how that flow goes. And he'll say, "Does that feel good, does that not feel good?" In some ways it can be a bit of a two-way thing. You'll say, "This doesn't feel quite right; how about if we did this?" And he'll say, "That looks good; do that . . ." and that kind of thing."

Twenty-three to twenty-six different ballets are performed by the Ailey company each season. Usually fifteen of these are choreographed by Alvin Ailey. The other pieces are choreographed by people whom Ailey invites to come in and work with his company, either reviving earlier works or creating entirely new ones on the company. This variety of choreographic talent challenges the dancers with a wide range of roles and styles.

Usually I learn the steps first, and then in my mind I take the steps and focus so intently that I can see exactly how I want to do them. That's really the most important thing, to envision yourself doing the part the way you really want it to look, like in a dream.

The training and the technical abilities of dancers keep improving as the overall level of dance intelligence spreads across the country. Benefiting from more professional schooling, each generation of dancers is more at ease with, for example, difficult movements and lifts, but the acceleration of technical facility creates and intensifies other problems.

You can do the steps with muscle memory, but once you get up on the stage, it's not about the steps at all. You really have to have a reason why you're doing it. You can't just go through the motions; it has to involve your whole self. Movement can't be labored and it can't be meaningless.

One easily overlooked pressure on the dancers comes from the push of younger dancers who have started to train at even earlier ages than the current generation of Ailey dancers, and so are ready to perform at a very young age. Another problem area emerges from the double-edged awareness of role interpretations that are important for artistic goals and for the development of a stage charisma. Dancers in the Ailey company now aspire to audience recognition, hoping to build an image similar to that of Judith Jamison, who became the first star of this non-star-oriented dance company.

Dudley Williams taught me I Want To Be Ready *about six months ago, and he's a magnificent teacher. He'd say "This is what the step is," and he would show me the step. Then he'd say "This is what I do because I've been doing it for ten or twelve years, and it's where I am in the evolution of my performance of this piece. That's not what the step was originally." Also, Dudley has a lot of imagery which Alvin gave him when he first taught him the part. When I teach the dance to a new member of the company, then I'll pass on those same images.*

When I dance Gazelle, *I don't try to mimic an animal; I just explore the animal within myself. Then, in the end, when the gazalle gets killed and it's sort of frantic, then I make it become whatever fear is haunting me."*

The financial underpinnings of the company, as in most dance companies, are always uncertain, but there is enough stability to continue the policy of inviting a variety of choreographers each season. As a way of thriving in this challenging environment, the dancers focus on their own personal artistic development, hoping there will be a chance for them to create a memorable role. And it does happen, as for example, Maxine Shulman's success in *Flowers*, and Dudley Williams's in *Love Songs*.

In dance there are many roles that are not specifically dramatic. But there is a sort of emotional kind of wash, like a hue or color, that comes through choreographically in the movements or through the music. So you just identify with the quality of the movement or whatever it means to you, or you just have the enjoyment of doing it or doing it well. And sometimes the dancer brings an idea or a sense of personal imagery to an abstract piece like Streams.

In Streams, *I'm a woman who, perhaps, is in this stream of water trying to move with it, or trying to move through it. Or I can take the idea that it's like life and that you try to move as smoothly as you can through everything.*

Alvin in particular has helped me make images. Whenever I feel I need one, I always ask him because he, obviously, had to have an image to choreograph the piece. So I want to try and get inside his head to see what he meant by a particular movement.

The dancers need more guidance and more rehearsal time, but there are a lot of ballets to rehearse. There is an element of learning by doing, and with each performance a dancer becomes more certain of his or her characterization of a role and its projection to the audience. Often, the problem is that some movement may feel right to the dancer doing it, but not come across with the same effect. It's a situation peculiar to all performing arts. Dancers, because they move quickly and because timing is such an important element, have little or no chance to cover up something that isn't quite right. It must be done right at the moment it is happening, because a gesture that may go unnoticed in day-to-day life is illuminated and intensified by a dancer's movement. In addition, the traditional perspective between the audience and the stage, while adding to the theatrical illusion of a performance, also magnifies movement so that the slightest gesture imparts an immediate visual, kinesthetic meaning to the audience.

Alvin has definitely helped me bring out a lot of things that I didn't really know were there.

There's been times when Alvin's told me that I've been totally boring and he's had me in tears. I was ready to quit; I was ready to take the first plane home. Once, it was after what I thought was one of the best performances that I've ever done. I talked to Dudley, though, and he's been in the company a long time. He said that Alvin used to tell him the same thing. It's one of his ways of making you work harder. Sometimes Alvin works in very strange ways.

Alvin Ailey has said that he carries with him vivid memories of his Texas childhood, including a strong desire to express himself. When he saw a poster advertising a Katherine Dunham concert, he became aware of a dance form that might interest him. Years later, he developed his own theatrical sense by working with Lester Horton in California and in Broadway shows in New York.

In many ways I learned how to dance from working in the company and with Ailey. Alvin was a dancer himself and he knows what dancers as artists need, and he tries to provide a climate in which people can grow, and evolve, and be challenged.

Part of a choreographer's job involves pulling a dancer out of his or her own self and into the created role. Since the choreographer has the image of what he wants projected firmly planted in his mind, he has to find a way for the dancers to realize this image through the movement that he is devising. It helps when the choreographer has a gift of psychological insight and enough practical experience of both life and dancers.

Alvin has so many sides, but he cares tremendously about the dancer. It's unusual, because from what I hear there are many choreographers who regard dancers as automatons you can plug in. And dancing is such a personal thing. If you're not treated as if you've got feelings, then there's a lot of hurt and you need a great deal of strength in order to overcome all the hurt and do the work. But Alvin is personal, and I think that's one of the reasons that he's been so successful. He's very personal in his choreography and in his relationships with people.

When Alvin Ailey started his company in 1958, he used a "pick-up" company of eight dancers that would meet to rehearse after finishing their regular jobs. His purpose, as he has stated, was "to awaken an appreciation of the trembling beauty of the Negro's cultural heritage through dance, through the exuberance of jazz, the ecstasy of spirituals and the dark rapture of blues."

Generally, what Alvin has tried to do with the company is to make dance accessible to everyone so that someone who has never seen dance before will enjoy the program, hopefully as much as someone who knows dance intimately. Though the way people will enjoy it will differ because of experience, education, eye, or what have you.

Usually audiences are very warm and responsive. They see something that has real gut feeling, and it releases something that maybe someone has been trying to hold in. In Japan we were told that audiences are very reserved, and in Taiwan, too. They're not used to showing their emotions, but people ran down to the stage. It was like a rock festival. I think it happens because they see dancers on the stage who are excited within themselves. If you're not excited, you can't convince anyone else of what you're doing.

Along the way between 1958 and 1979, Ailey got more and more involved with dance for its own sake, that is, dance as an art form. But he never forgot his original purpose.

I think Revelations *invariably provokes a wildly enthusiastic response wherever we've performed it, from Taiwan to Istanbul to London to Oklahoma. Still, there is something in the program that works for everyone. I think that's why we're so popular. I think we bring joy and people enjoy seeing us.*

The Alvin Ailey American Dance Theatre has traveled to six continents. They have danced in East and West Africa, Australia, the Near East, virtually every country in Europe, including the Soviet Union, and all across the United States as well as South America. It's hard on the dancers, but it fulfills the founding vision of the company, for the whole world has seen Ailey's message.

For us traveling can be very tiring, very grueling. In some ways it's a secure kind of thing because we only have performance responsibilities on the road. But traveling can get to be frustrating because it's such a sacrifice for something that's so simple; to dance and release energy through such a good way.

When the 1979 Capezio Award was given to Alvin Ailey, the accompanying citation expressed a thoughtful tribute. It cites him as: an actor-dancer, director of a company unprecedented in its impact throughout the world, and . . . a humanist who has interpreted the black heritage as a powerful expression common to all . . .''

There is no question about Ailey's popularity and influence with the general public. There is some question relating to the artistic level of the repertoire and its seriousness. Ailey critics say the company has found an easy, commercial way to attract people through its high-powered, flashy dancing to popular, strongly rhythmic music. It's a thorn that sticks lightly, but it does stick from time to time, as the dancers are well aware.

People sometimes say the Ailey company is too commercial and that our work isn't pure modern dance. I think that making entertainment and accessibility a negative association somehow makes the wrong equation between true art and accessibility.

As far as I'm concerned, Alvin's genius lies in his talent for theatricality, in his eye for dancers, and for his vision of what the company is and what it could be. That to me, is more valuable and more essential than simply his talent as a choreographer.

Entertainment, in its narrow sense, doesn't concern itself with unpleasant truths, but the Ailey repertoire, particularly in pieces like *Masekala Language* and *Rainbow Round My Shoulder*, focuses on themes depicting the destructive force of racial injustice. Fundamentally, the Alvin Ailey American Dance Theatre exists as an artistic voice representing the American black experience, but instead of preaching, the company reaches out to audiences through a vibrant depiction of the human situation. Alvin Ailey, in his role as choreographer/artistic director, understood that a theatricalized art, when clothed in velvet, can deliver a good-sized punch, while straight-out preaching can create resistance defeating his purpose, which is to engage the audience's understanding.

Finding Glen Tetley

I was in a position of accepting, not in a position of rejecting.

I WAS DELIGHTED TO HEAR that Glen Tetley was in New York City and that I would be able to arrange an interview with him. More often than not, Tetley is off in another part of the world, working with a dance company interested in expanding and modernizing its repertoire and its style of dancing. Since 1962, when the Netherlands Dance Theatre first invited him to Holland to choreograph for them, he has been traveling around the world bringing an individual, choreographic blend of modern dance and classical ballet to various international dance companies.

Tetley is not only interested in extending the physicality of the two dance techniques in his choreography, he is also concerned with experimenting with adventurous themes and with daring stage techniques. Working mostly with classical ballet companies in Europe, Tetley has, in a sense, played doctor, helping the European companies assimilate developments made by the twentieth-century American dance. He has placed many of these companies in the forefront of today's dance scene by injecting a modernism evolved out of his own contemporary dance background: extended sense of space; fluid, linked passage of movement; a broadened movement base flowing from dynamics such as contraction/release; sets designed as an integral part of a ballet; scores written by contemporary composers; innovative themes.

In an odd, unpredictable pattern, Tetley's work at first reversed the early nineteenth-century history of a nonexistent American dance culture borrowing from an old, sophisticated European tradition. Through his pioneering efforts in the 1960's, European dance absorbed the new American vitality. Now, in the last few years, the path has started to come full circle with an ever-growing interest in borrowing back innovations made by Americans working in the reawakened European dance world. American ballet companies, like American Ballet Theatre, are becoming more intrigued by Tetley's cross-fertilization of styles and by the work he has done with different companies, while younger choreographers follow in his footsteps.

Before Glen Tetley developed his present reputation as an iconoclastic choreographer, he had an unusually varied and successful career as a performer. An appealing, passionate dancer, he was one of the first solo-

Obvious graciousness and sensitivity. Glen Tetley (Photo: Anthony Crickmay)

ists to travel around the dance world: to Broadway for *Kiss Me Kate* and other productions; to TV for *Amahl and the Night Visitors*; and to work with a variety of concert dance companies. Then, after dancing with the New York City Opera Ballet in the early 1950's, he appeared as a soloist, performing with an extraordinary group of companies: the Martha Graham Dance Company, American Ballet Theatre, Jerome Robbins's Ballet U.S.A., the first Joffrey Ballet Company, John Butler's Company, as well as other smaller modern dance companies. Most talented dancers of that time—the 1950's through the 1960's—stayed primarily within one major discipline, even if their performing opportunities took them to different mediums. Tetley not only had the remarkable ability to perform well in these various styles of dance, he was interested in breaking through the tight aesthetic concepts that rigidly divided the traditional dance forms. This he did when, in 1962, he rented the auditorium of the Fashion Institute of Technology in New York and presented his first choreography. The result of his efforts at blending all the dance techniques, experiences, and concepts of his dance background was not entirely satisfactory. Overall reaction was mixed. One ballet, *Pierrot Lunaire*, was highly praised by John Martin in *The New York Times* and with that ballet Glen Tetley began his choreographic wanderings.

These facts about Glen Tetley's career were my lead material in developing questions for the interview. Thinking about them on my way to our scheduled appointment, I seemed to detect a restless quality in all this activity. Obviously, someone had to be a talented dancer to have the opportunity of performing with so many top companies. Most dancers, given the chance of dancing in the choreography of Martha Graham or Antony Tudor or Agnes De Mille, would have settled for the one major experience. Tetley had worked with almost every leading choreographer of the time, and then gone on. I wondered if it were possible that Tetley's multifaceted dance background reflected an idealized search for a perfect dance form. Perhaps, I hypothesized, Tetley was enacting the quest of a medieval knight; hunting for a perfect art is like searching for a holy grail. They are both idealistic, dedicated ventures that entail a variety of challenging events, and the goal remains a dream, attainable only for an instant before regaining its original ephemerality.

This notion brought to my mind a forgotten image from the ballet *Mutations*, which Glen Tetley had co-choreographed for the Netherlands Dance Theatre some years ago (Hans van Manaan co-choreographed the concurrent film). The work had been advertised as a nude ballet by the Brooklyn Academy of Music during a Netherlands Dance Theatre season in 1972. While the spicy copy brought in an overflow of patrons, the actual experience of nudity in *Mutations* had made the dancers appear more classically sculptural than brazenly scandalous. I remembered that the lone dancer in the opening solo had made me think of a medieval knight seen removing his armor. His costume was a pristine white body suit with gleaming metallic spools around each joint. As he stripped it off, he appeared more and more vulnerable, as though the loss of body covering stripped away both physical and emotional protection. I do not believe the intention of the costume had anything to do with an impression of a knight; it had probably been designed for its visual effect, not for any special symbolic meaning.

If there was any intended symbolism in *Mutations* it was, presumably, a statement about the body. There is always an immediate expressiveness inherent in our human physicality, and the art of dance springs from this obvious form of communication. Whether dance is clothed in the abstract purity of the classical technique or is a vehicle for a personal, expressive movement, the use of the human body as a visual, kinesthetic object is the essence of the dance experience. In *Mutations* the dancers, unprotected by even the briefest costume, had no visual image to project but their own nudity. While this nakedness effectively cast away traditional barriers between the audience and the dancers, it also depersonalized the dancers' individuality. They became perfect bodies with chiseled musculature, and as they moved through an essentially sculptured choreography, the clinical play of their muscles erased any obvious eroticism. Sensuality gave way to human anatomy.

Perhaps, I thought, Glen Tetley wanted the audience to go past its usual perception of nakedness, and of dancers. Not only had the dancers been naked, but they had come in close physical contact with the audience. A ramp, leading over the orchestra onto the stage, had been used with great effectiveness. The normal theatrical distance and perspective that clothes dancers with the magic of illusion disintegrated in the physical proximity of the sweaty, hard-working women and men. For some people sitting in the orchestra, it was possible to reach up to the ramp and touch a performer's foot. The closeness had a startling effect. It wasn't only the dancers who had been stripped of an illusive covering, the entire communication of a dance experience had been stripped to its essential physical communication.

Since I was now five minutes away from our meeting place, I decided to forget this labyrinth of labels and aesthetics. There were too many new works to be discussed. Altogether Tetley has choreographed some thirty ballets for almost as many different companies. In addition to *Mutations* he has created *Circles, Sargasso, The Anatomy Lesson, Arena*, and *Imaginary Film* for the Netherlands Dance Theatre; *Field Figures* and *Laborintus* for the Royal Ballet in England; *Mythical Hunters* for Batsheva Company of Israel; *Gemini* for the Australian Ballet; *Chronochrome* for the Hamburg State Opera; *Le Sacre du Printemps* for the Munich State Opera Ballet; and many other ballets including *Rag Dances, Ziggurat, Tristan, Sphinx, Ricercare, Embrace Tiger & Return to Mountain*. He has worked with Ballet Rambert, the Stuttgart Ballet, American Ballet Theatre, the Festival Ballet, and the official ballet companies of Sweden, Denmark, and Finland. In addition to choreographing for these different companies, Tetley has had his own dance company; he has been artistic director of the Netherlands Dance Theatre, and after John Cranko died, he directed the Stuttgart Ballet Company for two years.

Reality, even in a prepared interview, has a way of sweeping abstract questions away. At first, when I actually meet Glen Tetley, I begin by asking what I had come to believe was a leading question. What I hadn't taken into account in my meandering thoughts was the human personality—the physicality which colors and shades conversations. Charmed by his obvious graciousness and sensitivity, I decided my theoretical questions were entirely out of context. I tucked them away for another time, sat back, and listened to Tetley's soft voice carefully describing the same facts that I had so diligently reviewed in my notes and in the clippings file of the Dance Research Library. As the minutes went by, it occurred to me that Tetley's quick, eager smile was as good an explanation as any for his on-going dance quest. By the time our conversation had finished, I was convinced that if I had told him of my hypothetical analysis of his choreographic traveling as a restless search for perfection, his blue eyes would at first register a moment's surprise. Then he would chuckle and reply, "In January, I'll be working in the Netherlands. . . ."

e.r. *I was fascinated by a recent statement of yours in which you said that you felt an affinity with the music of Stockhausen, Webern, and Berg, because, like you, they're working with a nineteenth-century romantic sensibility and twentieth-century forms. Do you see the romantic sensibility as one that focuses on expressing personal feeling about existence?*

g.t. I know I'm a very romantic person. I'm not a person who lives in the past: the ideal of many early romantic artists. I believe there is the possibility of being a romantic person even in our terrifying day.

e.r. *Do you think your choreography, with its fusion of modern dance and classical ballet, is the practical application of your feelings about updating the romantic sensibility?*

g.t. I started in dance late and I've been drawn to works which intrigued me, not only because of their emotional and physical impact, but because of their strong sense of form. I was trained in medicine and come from a scientific background. Originally, I had a great interest in going into the field of medicine, but I also felt it would be difficult for me to shutter my entire life off from emotion. When I was going through a crisis about dealing with this creative urge, and yet staying in medicine, a wonderful anatomy professor at Franklin and Màrshall College said, "Maybe you can do both, because Oliver Wendell

Holmes, for example, was both a famous writer and a doctor; and there have been many doctors who have done this as well." I finally left medicine and went into the dance, but I did find that the two worlds do go beautifully hand in hand. That is, the scientific world or the world of structure, and the emotional, interior world, which is the romantic view of things. So I really started to be involved in that form/emotion bipolarity even before I came into dance.

e.r. *You felt that dance enabled you to pull both sides together?*

g.t. When I first started studying dance, I had the good luck to begin with Hanya Holm, who had been a disciple of the German modern dancer Mary Wigman. Hanya had a precise, scientific grasp of what pure movement could be and I loved studying with her. I loved how she analyzed the way the body moves: both in its physical relationship to space and in the principles of technique. She analyzed a *plié* and a *relevé* and a *battement* and so forth in terms of basic structural movement, not just stylistic movement. Hanya's teaching was directed toward understanding the physical basis of what was happening in the body during these different movements.

e.r. *That would have meshed with your earlier anatomy studies.*

g.t. Yes. Hanya was also working with the concept of movement as being centrifugal and/or centripetal. This approach to movement came out of the laboratory and I understood these ideas. But, at the same time, I was enormously struck by Martha Graham's work. When I first came to New York, in the late '40's, there was a wonderful ferment among all of these strong, pioneer leaders who were then working at their heights. It was terribly exciting. You felt always as if you were on the brink of discovering something because they were discovering something and you were discovering something with them. Hanya was discovering analysis of movement and space. Martha was stripping the language of theatre right down to its very strong elemental bones. She was doing extraordinary things. There was a wonderful Puritan quality to Martha's work: a puritanism of movement, but a richness at the same time. I think, emotionally, I wanted to bc with Martha and maybe, also, with her technique. There again the sense of the technique is beautiful. Martha took from so many elements and structured them to make one wonderful vocabulary.

e.r. *I always felt that the Graham technique was very beautiful, very logical.*

g.t. Yes, extraordinary. What a wonderful teacher Martha has been. Once you feel that, you always go back to those beginnings. Just the way she starts each class, directing your concentration on the emptying out of breath. You start communicating about the body's breath. It's a beautiful beginning for a performer's work or for someone who is creating choreography. I always go back to that beginning of releasing breath as a way of feeling my energy when I start choreographing, start making dance movements. But I was one of those people who from the beginning were interested in both the classical ballet and the modern dance. Even though I was living right inside the nests of the pioneers, that is, Hanya and Martha . . . and I worked with Charles Weidman, Doris Humphrey. . . .

e.r.   You have a most unusual background.

g.t.   You know, we didn't have any money in those early days. We had nothing. None of the modern dance companies could sustain an ongoing company, so you had to go to many places, do many things. You had to accept and go after all these various experiences.

e.r.   Practicality has a way of influencing one's life direction.

g.t.   I started studying dance very late and so I started studying classical ballet because I wanted all experiences. I studied with Antony Tudor and Margaret Craske because I wanted to know the Cecchetti system. I also went to the School of American Ballet and studied with the wonderful Russians: Oboukhov and Vladimirov. I was in a position of accepting, not in a position of rejecting anything. I think I was possibly the first principal dancer to be performing simultaneously in classical ballet with American Ballet Theatre and with Martha Graham in her own, opposite technique.

e.r.   Did you find that difficult in terms of your body? Were there problems in relating to space or to centering? I mean as a dancer, not in terms of ideas.

g.t.   It's difficult in that perhaps one world is asking for more gravity and one world is asking for more air. If you're working specifically with the classical technique, then you're studying every day to defeat gravity and it's hard to get that feeling that movement has weight and leads into the floor. It's just a question of adapting yourself in a rehearsal to things which are diametrically opposed.

e.r.   I think it's one of those things that are easier said than done.

g.t.   I think, today, that we're reaching that point of flexibility in dance. There has been so much exploration of dance in this century and so much done in terms of pushing technique that we're evolving the genus dancers who can do everything and have no problems at all. Someone like Baryshnikov has no problems as a dancer because his prodigious technique frees him. And freedom is the purpose of technique. It's ironic; one becomes natural in dance through a lot of arduous training.

e.r.   In discussing your choreography, I believe that you've said you didn't want to create a movement false to the theme or emotion of a particular ballet. That's basically a modern dance idea.

g.t.   When I began to choreograph, I recognized the difference between Martha Graham's technique and Martha Graham's theatrical vocabulary. One has to model oneself on other people, but I don't think I've ever choreographed in Martha's style. I think I've used the elements of her technique, certainly, and still do. But I've never choreographed a Graham ballet, a Balanchine ballet, or a Tudor ballet. These are all genius creators that I admire very much. Hanya once said to me that each of us has our own particular sense of rhythm, our own movement qualities, and we're each that little bit different. I think as a choreographer you have to find that sense of difference and stay within it. It's not a limitation, because it's going deeper and deeper into yourself. If you're honest, you find a way for others to see into your work, and you find the way you want dancers to move in your work.

e.r. *There's a wide range of styles and themes in your work. I know that each of your ballets that I've seen is very different. For example,* Pierrot Lunaire *focuses on a few characters and* Voluntaries *is a large group work without a plotted story. I mention these two works because they're two of my favorite Glen Tetley ballets.*

g.t. Pierrot Lunaire was the first ballet that I did.

e.r. *You must have been interested in the whole idea of Harlequin and that early period of commedia dell'arte pantomime. Do you usually start a ballet with an idea?*

g.t. I think it comes from many directions. With *Pierrot*, the first thing that absolutely struck me off my feet was the sound of the Schönberg score of the same name, Pierrot Lunaire. It was so extraordinary, so unusual; it's unlike any other score. Even after some sixty odd years, it's still too contemporary for some people. However; I responded kinesthetically to that music, and emotionally I felt there was something in it that I wanted to relate to. Also the figure of the introverted clown, Pierrot, intrigued me; and I liked the fact that Schönberg hadn't made him a stereotype character. In his version, Pierrot isn't aware of the fact that he's being observed and that he's spilling his insides out. He's a tortured person: someone who's swinging all the time from enormous highs to enormous lows. I identified with what Pierrot was going through. Also, Hanya Holm had cast me as Harlequin in the Broadway production of *Kiss Me Kate*, so I'd already danced a version of the character and studied the traditional pantomime movement. And when I was a child, I had been interested in puppets and marionettes. I wanted to layer all of these impressions and experiences in one ballet. *Pierrot* was intriguing to do because there were so many levels. I decided the vocabulary should be commedia, but because Pierrot also comes out of the classical world, I used the classical vocabulary as a base for his movement. Pierrot was also a figure of *angst* and his movement had to show exactly where he'd been, so it came out of all the contemporary movement that I had studied. I worked with some deep solar plexus movement for Pierrot, and, hopefully, all these elements blended together. Since Pierrot is sometimes called the poet of the acrobats, I did want him high up in the air, but not in the balletic use of that space. For a figure who was experiencing such highs and lows, I didn't want to use the air alone, which is the space of the classical ballet, nor did I want just the floor space of the contemporary dance. The problem was solved when Rouben Ter-Arutunian designed a scaffolding for me to use as a prop for Pierrot. Throughout the dance Pierrot goes from swinging on the highest bars to inhabiting the lowest part of the floor.

e.r. *As I recall, the ballet was constructed through a series of images of events in Pierrot's life.*

g.t. The structure of the music interested me and influenced my whole approach to the structure of the ballet. I'm always conditioned and excited and inspired by the music. In the Schönberg score there aren't any long phrases. He states his themes concisely. He uses little repetition, but there are extremes of sudden, fast tempos, and there are slow tempos that happen quickly, and then that rhythm's broken, too. Another score, like the score for *Voluntaries*—Concerto for Organ, Strings, and Percussion, a concerto which to me is one of Poulenc's best scores—takes me to the opposite extreme. That's an inward score with a beautiful sensibility of lyricism and a deep religious feeling. Poulenc is a man of the theatre and he's a man of the church and you feel it in this score. When I did *Voluntaries*, I was working with the Stuttgart Company, a classical ballet company with great dancers such as Marcia Haydee, Richard Cragun, and Brigette Keill. The movement had to come out of their bodies; it had to be elevated, to be on pointe, and to be in the classical vocabulary. The ballet has a linear quality and a script with a feeling of a story. However, I would never want to do the same ballet over and over again. Each time, I've wanted to do a work that would solve a particular problem. I've wanted to go into an area, tackle it completely, and then having done it, go on and do something else. I've gone into many diverse areas, always, hopefully, in my own way.

e.r. *When you did* Pierrot *in 1962, the lines were still quite sharply drawn between the techniques and the aesthetic concepts of modern dance and those of the classical ballet.*

g.t. It's strange. I think my working in this area of both ballet and modern dance has been intuitive, but it seems that I was needed. When the Netherlands Dance Theatre was first forming as a company, they were interested in using the techniques of American contemporary

"The ballet has a linear quality and a script with the feeling of a story." Natalia Makarova in **Voluntaries** *(Photo: Martha Swope)*

dance with those of the classical ballet. The company was having a repertoire created for them and they wanted me to come and work with them because of my background in American contemporary dance, and because I was both a performer and a choreographer in the classical tradition as well. At the time the Netherlands Dance Theatre was beginning, there wasn't a company in this country that was forming a repertoire based on that approach. Since the beginnings of my own dance career, that bipolarity had been with me, and the majority of my work has been from that orientation. Since choreographing for the Netherlands Dance Theatre, I've worked with many classical companies.

e.r.   *I know you've choreographed for companies all over the world. I should think the variety would be interesting but also a challenge, because each company must have a different personality and a different way of moving. It must be stimulating, though it could be difficult to constantly reestablish yourself.*

g.t.   It can be terrifying to walk into a totally strange company to do what is an intimate act: creating for people and with people. I'm not so courageous anymore. About ten years ago I was working with the Royal Ballet (England) for the first time and Jerry Robbins, whom I know and like very much, was there. He asked me if I was setting an old work on the company or doing a new work. When I told him that I was doing a new work, he said that either I was extremely brave or out of my mind. Actually, the Netherlands was a home country for me. I've lived in Holland and I like it there, and when I was working with the Netherlands Dance Theatre, I made friends that I've had ever since. Even with my peripatetic existence, I've kept solid roots here in New York. I've lived in the city for thirty-six years and I've kept the same apartment for twenty-two of those years, even during periods of my working with companies in other countries.

e.r.   *Since you've done so many ballets with different companies and in various countries, how do you remember them? When you set one of your ballets on a new company, how do you remember what you've done? Do you have it written down, and also do you get different interpretations with each company?*

g.t.   I'm choosy about the companies I work with. Actually, there are only certain companies that I work with and I've set up a close relationship with each of them: the Netherlands Dance Theatre, Ballet Rambert, the Royal Ballet (England), American Ballet Theatre, and somehow Scandinavia. I've had close association with the Royal Danish, Royal Swedish, and the Royal Norwegian Ballet companies. I feel at home with these companies because I've gone back so many times. In the early days, I could remember the ballets that I had done because I hadn't done that many. I used film then and I made personal notes.

Now I'm close to the Benesh system of choreology. I'm one of their patrons and all of my ballets are notated in Benesh. When I go to work with a company, I go with an assistant who is a choreologist and has the entire score notated right with the music score, and it's wonderful. It's impossible to remember all the details in your head. The Benesh scores are very complete. The choreologist has worked with me from the beginning of the ballet, which is the best way as she is aware of all the variants that can be used in setting the ballet. When I set a ballet on one or two companies, the variants come with how individuals do the steps. Notation is an enormous help because you can quickly set the material and then use the majority of the time to change, adapt, and rechoreograph where it's necessary. I think every ballet needs its choreographer there. Again, a dance isn't something that stays perfect. You have to go back again and again and rehearse and re-rehearse. . . . It's quite an effort to keep it alive, to keep it going.

e.r. *And you prefer the Benesh to the Laban system?*

g.t. I studied Laban notation, but I like Benesh better because there's an utter simplicity to its symbolic language. Like the music symbols, Benesh uses only a few symbols, but they can be manipulated to infinity. We're blessed now in having more than one method of recording. Videotape is good, but there's nothing so correct as a notation score, and it doesn't break down the rehearsal structure. With videotape or film you have to bring in a machine and get it working. The dancers relax and it's difficult to reestablish the same atmosphere.

e.r. *Are you doing something new at the moment? I know that last spring you did* The Tempest *for England's Ballet Rambert and* Contradances *for American Ballet Theatre. Two different companies and two very different ballets. One revolves around a famous play and the other deals with the materials of dance.*

g.t. I really enjoyed working on *Contradances*. It was the beginning of the season; we had total concentration, and it was one of the best rehearsal periods I've ever had. I created a ballet specifically for the two great dancers Natalia Makarova and Anthony Dowell. I wanted to use their specific movement qualities and also the speed and brilliance of the American Ballet Theatre corps. I worked with an exciting, fascinating Webern score (Opus 1, 5, 6). He starts with a romantic passacaglia in Opus 1, and by Opus 6 he's modified that language very, very much; he's distilled it, he's concentrated it, he's minimized it, and so on. Much of the movement came out in passionate dancing.

e.r. *By chance?*

g.t. I took a cue from the fact that Opus 1 is a passacaglia. I'm kind of intrigued by how the passacaglia had evolved. It was called a passionate dance when it came out and was considered immoral.

e.r. *Things have changed.*

g.t. We identify it with Bach—the Bach Passacaglia; but actually it was the period when the formal dance of the court suddenly had a new direction. It went from two/four to three/four and for them at that time it was a huge shift in rhythm and in passion. Webern's passacaglia starts out calmly and then it begins, suddenly, to take off in these wild flights of passion. I really enjoyed working on it. I also enjoyed working with Makarova and Dowell, both of whom have unbelievable gifts. They dance faster than anybody and they can also be absolutely still. . . .

e.r. *The Tempest came after the period with ABT?*

g.t. I went to England to prepare it. I must say it was one of the most concentrated experiences I have ever had. It took three-and-a-half months of going to the studio every day and knowing that every day I had to finish so many minutes for each day. If I'm working well, I usually produce ten minutes a day, but this was a three-and-a-half-hour production so I needed about eighteen minutes a day, and my concentration lasts for about four hours of intensive work. Sometimes, when things don't quite come, I've learned to rely on craft and that takes me through a working period. *The Tempest* is a beautiful play for dance because it's so full of symbolism; it's not the action of the story which is meaningful as much as what it symbolizes. I wanted to see if I could do the Shakespeare story without breaking it down into a typical, nineteenth-century Russian balletic stylization in which the play is really just a vehicle for a series of variations and pas de deux, pas de trois, pas de quatres, pas des six. In preparing the ballet, I worked closely with the composer and the designer. I said to Arne Nordheim, the composer, that "first of all, you have to make good musical sense of the play and then I can make good choreographic sense." I wanted to find a language for the dance that could speak and sustain the work, but not stop the action for the virtuosity, which is an exciting part of the ballet. After a long search, which included seeing productions of the play, I decided to work around the magical elements of Caliban and Ariel. I used the main characters: Prospero, Miranda, Ferdinand, and Caliban and Ariel to carry the story, emphasizing the overall symbolic dimension of the characters. For example, I saw Miranda not only as the Duke's daughter, but as a symbol of innocence. Ballet Rambert is a small company that is based on the classical ballet, but they don't work on pointe. Since we were working with a small company, and probably on small stages, I thought that we should work with an economy of means as they do in the oriental theatre. So I used elements of oriental theatre in the staging and in the movements.

We also used lots and lots of china silk, but probably or mostly because it's one of the cheapest materials you can buy. I was wiped out after the production. I'm beginning to come back to life now.

e.r. *Will you set* The Tempest *on another company?*

g.t. The composer, Arne Nordheim, is Scandinavia's leading contemporary composer. He lives in Oslo, and I've just agreed to do a production of the ballet with the Norwegian State Opera. We're going to start rehearsals next May and open in September 1980. The work is all there now, but I'm happy to be able to stage it again. It's a chance to try some new things and to make some changes in it, which I'm going to do.

e.r. *Is there any new music that has captured your fancy?*

g.t. I'll be going to Holland in January to do a new piece for the Netherlands Dance Theatre. I haven't been back there for some years. Unless I'm working in advance with a designer or a composer, I don't like to talk about a new work before I've started working on it.

e.r. *Is it just an idea until you start working on it?*

g.t. I don't like to talk about a new work too much before I start on it because then it starts to get crystallized. It seems to take a direction before I've started to work on it.

I've just set my ballet, *Sphinx*, for the Festival Ballet (England). If you stay in the dance world long enough, you begin to see and work with some of the same people; even though they might be in different companies. You work so closely with one another; it's very stimulating. I like the dance world.

e.r. *Something that has always completely fascinated me about dance is the expressiveness of the body as a way of communicating. For example, arms can say so much; but the expressiveness isn't only on the stage. You can see it when you watch people on a social dance floor. People don't realize how much of themselves they reveal through movement or gesture, but that's another aspect.*

g.t. I love that. I'm a great people watcher. It's the most fascinating thing in the world just to walk out on the streets of New York. You don't need any other entertainment. I did one of my famous walks the other day. Every once in a while I get this great urge to walk a lot. The other day I went to an exhibition of a sculptor and a painter that one of the dancers is having in his apartment. Afterwards, I walked from his house at Eighty-First Street and Columbus Avenue down to Fifth Avenue and Ninth Street. That's a long walk through all the different qualities of New York life.

e.r. *And it ends up on the stage . . . in some way . . . in your work?*

g.t. Maybe.

Encounter with Twyla Tharp

I want something substantial, something of substance.

Twyla tharp and her group of dancers are giving a lecture-demonstration in a New York University gymnasium. It is the winter of 1970, and the demonstration is part of a course given at NYU by Harvey Lichtenstein, the newly appointed director of the Brooklyn Academy of Music. I've been away from New York City and from the dance world for many years, and am now at the point of reentry via a job at *Dance Magazine* and this short overview course on modern dance. A friend of mine who teaches dance comes with me to these weekly lectures. She is interested in hearing what topic Harvey will select to comment on. Harvey has selected Twyla Tharp.

Entering the gym, we find seats on the bleachers. Harvey tells us, "Twyla Tharp is one of the most exciting young choreographers around today." Tonight, she and her group will do a section of their piece, *Group Activities*. Wearing sneakers and dressed in layers of tights, warm-up shirts, and leg warmers, the five young women and Twyla come onto the gymnasium floor and go into their first formation of two uneven parallel lines in the center of the floor space. I look, and I don't believe what I am seeing. The "most exciting young choreographer," and her dancers appear to be a group of self-propelled Tinker Toys who test their joints with quick, subtle movements of their arms and legs. I am slightly bewildered by their activity and ask myself, is this dance—are they dancing?

The dancers, grim-faced and concentrating, provide their own accompaniment by counting aloud. Now and again a phrase is spoken out by one of the girls, then picked up by another dancer in the group. In the same way, movement seems to be relayed from one dancer to another. There appears to be a choreographed, but seemingly improvisational, plan based on movement impulses that are simultaneously sent out by one or more of the dancers, picked up, converted, held, and then passed on to another one or more of the group. In the midst of this complex activity, I see individual dancers, as loose as Raggedy-Ann dolls, propelling their obviously well trained bodies through incredible backward turns. No one seems to be dancing in any sort of unison, and I find it hard to follow the movement phrasing. Slowly, as the dancers continue to group, break, regroup, count, talk, and turn, I begin to have some inkling of what they are up to.

A witty sense of humor and an observant eye. Twyla Tharp (Photo: Lois Greenfield)

As I watch, increasingly fascinated by what I am seeing, my sensibility is nudged by the visual impression of an intensely serious group of dancers revealing a plan well known to them, but so difficult for an outsider to follow. From somewhere in my own inner world comes a vision of these very up-to-date young women superimposed over a mythic group, perhaps Cretan, solemnly participating in an ancient, ritualistic team sport. But this is only a moment's fancy. In the NYU gym, Twyla Tharp is the team's captain, and the game the dancers are really playing is freeing the vocabulary of movement from the rigidity of any one specific dance technique. And the rules, as I see them, require the dancers to respond to each other's movement signals through highly structured time sequences; in effect, they are reproducing something like a very sophisticated version of the plays given in a football huddle.

This kind of teamwork requires each dancer to have superb technical control and a lot of time for group rehearsal hours. Altogether, an immense effort of both time and energy is involved in creating these dances. Given the economic conditions of working in the avant-garde of dance, I am not surprised to hear Twyla tell us after the demonstration: "I am thinking of disbanding this group because I can only pay the dancers two dollars a week. This means that the girls have to work some place else to earn money to live. They rehearse and perform with me without any reimbursement for their time and effort. I would like to be able to pay them for their dancing."

It is one year later, 1971, and I am producing "Dance Focus." I both choose and interview the people appearing on this radio program, and, intrigued by what I have seen of Twyla Tharp's work at the New York University lecture-demonstration, I decide to do a program about Twyla and her dancers while they are at work in their studio.

When I call the studio, Sara Rudner, one of the group's most talented dancers, answers the telephone. "Sure, we'd love to do the program, but Twyla is living upstate on a farm. She only comes into the city from time to time."

The dance season is busy. I go on to other things. Twyla has a baby. Sara and I have a few more pleasant telephone calls; the program is never made.

In October 1972, Twyla Tharp and her dancers are performing at New York City's ANTA Theatre as part of the American Dance Marathon. Organized by modern dance producer Charles Reinhart, the marathon, or festival of dance, gives eighteen modern dance companies a one- or two-performance "season" in a Broadway house. There are two or three companies on each evening's program, and the Twyla Tharp Dance Company is sharing its program with the Erick Hawkins Dance Company.

A new Tharp piece, *Raggedy Dances*, is performed by Twyla and her company, which now includes one male dancer. A long, rambling ballet, it is built on the syncopated rhythms of Scott Joplin's rag music, which in an unexpected way create a recognizable foundation for those inscrutably complex movement patterns that Tharp devises. Add costumes with a fashion look, and the Tharp choreography becomes a comment on American social manners both on and off the dance floor.

In the midst of the ballet is a solo, *The Entertainer*, that Twyla has choreographed for herself to Joplin's 1902 piece of the same name. Dressed in a purple bikini, she uses all of her compact 5-foot-3-inch body to portray her "entertainer," a vulnerable, manipulative, seductive, and disarmingly indifferent character. As she wriggles and slithers to those pulsating ragtime sounds, her looseness masks a very deft physical performance, but I'm not sure whether her slightly haughty attitude is part of the *Entertainer's* character, or simply Twyla being Twyla Tharp.

By chance, at intermission, I meet Barbara from WBAI's Free Music Store. Barbara is all smiling enthusiasm, "Isn't she great? I love that company. They're really first class, the best." The audience, young, responsive, and in Twyla's camp, is tuned into the language of the Tharp dancers. In fact, it is becoming clearer and clearer that from all those seemingly disconnected wriggles that Tharp is emerging as a choreographer with a witty sense of humor and an observant eye.

Who is Twyla Tharp? My first impression of her made me think of the early photographs of Isadora Duncan. Why? I'm not sure. Her biography says simply that she was born in Portland, Indiana, in 1941 and moved to San Bernardino, California, as a child. It further states that the source of her unusual name stems from a newspaper clipping that her mother saw and copied. There is no mention of Isadora Duncan. She came to New York to study art history at Barnard College. After graduation, she stayed on in New York to dance and to choreograph.

After seeing *Raggedy Dances*, I renew my attempt to get in touch with Twyla Tharp in the hope of arranging that radio interview we never did. Yes, she is back from the farm and in the city now, but no, she is extremely busy choreographing a ballet for the Joffrey Ballet Company.

Deuce Coupe is the name of the ballet that Twyla choreographs for the Joffrey. The ballet's music is a taped selection of songs by the Beach Boys, a rock group, and the set is a backdrop painted on stage by a group of kids with spray cans who call themselves the United Graffiti Artists. Twyla's own company mixes on stage with the members of the Joffrey Company, while at the same time, one lone Joffrey dancer goes through the entire classical ballet vocabulary in counterpoint to the overall action, which is Tharp's dry, witty choreographic comment on youthful America. The two companies mix surprisingly well and the ease of the dancers belies the deftness of the choreography and the truth of the insights.

It is March 1, 1973. *Deuce Coupe* is a big, every-seat-sold-out hit. Twyla Tharp is a star.

On the theory that you run with the ball when you can, the Joffrey Ballet Company asks Twyla Tharp to choreograph another ballet for them. Twyla, who has a knack for titles, as well as ballets, comes up with *As Time Goes By* for the Joffrey's 1973 fall season. Set to Haydn's music, this new ballet proves to be as witty and brazen as a blare from a French horn.

Working only with dancers from the Joffrey Ballet Company, Tharp uses *As Time Goes By* to explore further her own relationship to classical ballet. She first creates the calm center which is the core of the classical ballet idiom, and then, like a naughty child asking, "Is this really all dance can do?" knocks everything off center with slight, expressive hip thrusts, shoulder shrugs, and subtle, quick, off-center balances. Her overall choreographic statement continues to hinge, as it has from her earliest work, on viewing each dancer as an individual. This means, for example, that when six dancers are on stage in *As Time Goes By*, there are six solo performers dancing at the same time, in the same place, but with six different movement and rhythmic patterns. It is distracting at first, but settles down as the patterns emerge. In juxtaposition to the rest of the program, the originality of *As Time Goes By* glows with an embarrassing brilliance.

I am working on a series highlighting choreographers, and when I read that one of the critics does not find *As Time Goes By* to be a real, "classical" ballet, I call Twyla. "Would you like to come and talk about what makes a real ballet?" Twyla says, "I don't want to talk about *As Time Goes By*." I say, "The series is about choreography. I assume that most radio listeners don't know too much about dance, and choreography is a mystifying process." Twyla agrees to do the interview, and we arrange the time, the day, and I give her WBAI's address.

The radio station is housed in a converted church, and on the steps outside, Twyla and I meet formally for the first time. "Follow me," I say, as I lead her past the garbage cans and down a flight of stairs. "I'll only ask you questions about your work. We'll record on tape and later I'll edit it. O.K.?"

"O.K." We make our way up a flight of stairs and down a corridor into the back of the church where the sound studios have been built.

e.r. Twyla, every time I see your work, I'm more and more fascinated by it. I was looking through some newspaper clippings in preparing for today, and found one reviewer who uses three adjectives that I thought very apt. They are "original," "intense," and "compel-

ling." I think those same adjectives can be applied equally to your dancing and to your choreography. It's easy to forget that a choreographer is often a dancer as well, and this is certainly most true with you. You could have settled into a career as a dancer.

t.t. Well, a lot of choreographers tend to forget they are dancers for a very good reason; it's really not possible to do both for very long with the decisions that have to be made. I guess there's always tension between the two, and that tension is part of what gives a performer who also does the dance-making, or a performer who is involved with the creation of whatever the show may be, a certain intensity. It's the kind of intensity that is usual with the dichotomy between performing and creating.

e.r. *Being part of something and knowing that you have done it?*

t.t. Between trying to see and trying to do; I guess, that is the problem.

e.r. *Are you set now in the direction of choreography, or do you slide back and forth?*

t.t. I become very unhealthy when I'm not really dancing, because first of all, I don't feel well physically, and second of all, it's just something that I have done for so long that it's confusing to me not to dance, but I just don't seem to have time any more. I haven't been to class for about five months, and I'm working to get in a barre about three times a week.

e.r. *When you take class, what do you usually take, ballet?*

t.t. Ballet class.

e.r. *What is your background in dance?*

t.t. Very eclectic, total eclecticism.

e.r. *Which means everything.*

t.t. Everything. From the age of four in garages and neighborhood dancing schools.

e.r. *You danced with Paul Taylor at one point, which means that somewhere in there is a modern dance background.*

t.t. I danced with Paul Taylor's company for one year, that was the only performing I did with a company other than my own.

e.r. *Did you ever study with Merce Cunningham?*

t.t. Quite a bit. About two years.

e.r. *For curiosity's sake, are you at all interested or involved with what he is doing? Have you found yourself influenced by him in any way?*

t.t. Yes, Merce is a master teacher. He really has a comprehension of what it means to teach, which is apart from knowing about dancing. It happens that he teaches dancing, but that is almost beside the point when one sees Merce teach. He has something enormously rare and really wonderful. And in his work, Merce has a capability for making performing itself into storytelling in a way that is not as subjective as performers tend to become. I think what it is, is the objectivity that makes Merce's work so distinctive, and perhaps my company is influenced by that. My company is fortunate; it's not very large, but it is nonetheless filled with people who are willing to take the responsibility, not just for themselves, but for every other member of the company, which means that a dancer doing one of our pieces not only knows her or his part, but knows everyone else's part who is working at the same time, and knows how that fits into the whole work. I mean, it's an honor and a responsibility, and it's something few dancers seem to take seriously. Musicians are much better about it because harmony is easier to hear than it is to see.

e.r. *Do you mean the responsibility the dancers have to be aware of other people dancing at the same time?*

t.t. To realize and acknowledge their importance relative to your own, not to just maintain what you are doing and to put that out front, but to know. I mean, it's like any kind of good team-work, passing the ball third man back, and you don't get any place near the hoop, but everyone still knows what put it into the hoop.

e.r. *Then the interaction among the dancers on stage is important to you. And from what I've seen of your work, not only their movement in space, but the exploration of the quality that each dancer has when moving.*

t.t. Oh, yes. That's why Balanchine is such a marvelous choreographer. He has a concept of his dancers that means to me that he knows each of them so well that he can propose something for them to try that they might not be aware that they can do. There's always a wonderful kind of excitement about the dancers recognizing something of themselves that they sense, but had never really brought to the fore, and I think it is that quality that audiences can respond to. You only get it by comprehending something about the specific performer. I have seen some of Balanchine's dancers in class; it's almost shocking to see how little concept they have of themselves as dancers in relation to how much he has of them. He sees them architecturally, in a way that I think is unique. He is so aware of what physicality can produce, and what different sorts of physicalities can produce, and just what a long arm can do. I mean, he's challenged himself with the specifics of dancers, which is something I find choreographers reluctant to do. They are fast to form generalizations about individual dancers and stick to it, but Balanchine doesn't do this.

e.r. *We can add Balanchine as an influence on your work, then. In your last piece,* As Time Goes By, *I loved watching the way you move people around the stage. You don't use set, predictable patterns in your grouping of dancers. I didn't know from second to second what I was going to see on the stage next; in which direction the dancer would go; how the group would form or dissolve. There was a marvelous element of surprise, and the stage was very alive.*

t.t.   You saw it only one time?

e.r.   *I saw it only one time.*

t.t.   So you couldn't say which is the important part. That's O.K., but it's more important to me that on seeing a piece a second or third time, that what was at first a surprise remains a surprise, but that the logic of it comes across, that it's not just arbitrary.

e.r.   *Well, I understand there's a flow. I did find that the second time I saw your ballet,* Deuce Coupe, *I found it richer; the surprise had deepened. I did notice that in* Deuce Coupe, *you use movement to reveal people's attitudes, which is a subtle form of characterization. But what really fascinates me about your work, and what I think is truly original, is your use of movement, the way the dynamics start off at any one point in the body and then ripple through legs, or arms, or torso, or it seems everything all at once.*

t.t.   Speaking beyond the movement for each individual dancer, is the movement throughout the whole piece, and throughout all the parts that make the structure. And that to me, particulary in *As Time Goes By*, is the important thing. For example, Beatrice Rodriguez [Joffrey Ballet Company] opens the thing with a solo. She is joined by twelve dancers, who act as a very large group, which then filters out, bit by bit, down to a smaller number of dancers once again, which continues filtering down to one dancer. So, we go from one dancer through a whole variety of tension points back down to one dancer, but along the way, the movement quality changes entirely. Her beginning is very springy and tightly coiled, and like steel, and it works through all these different angles. "Angles" is not a word that I'm particularly fond of abstractly, I like it concretely, but the movement works through all these angles down to a quality of movement that is just the opposite, which is almost dissipated, which has so little tension to it that it's just flowing out of the finger tips. It happened that the two dancers who were chosen to quote, portray, if you will, these kinds of movements, were the wrong sex, which was an interesting problem to me. Ordinarily, one would associate maleness with that first quality, and femaleness with lyricism. But Larry Grenier [Joffrey Ballet Company] was called to rehearsal one day; I was going to do something entirely different with the last section, and I started working with him, and he showed me that he was a really unique lyric dancer. And I was dumbfounded, and I just sat there and said, "Can I believe my eyes? Is this as exceptional as I feel it is? Is this really such a fine male lyric dancer?" So, Bea was also available to me, and I had worked with her in *Deuce Coupe* in which she danced a little number called *Wouldn't It Be Nice?* In it she had a clarity, and a precision, and really a steely brilliance, and an edge and a faceting to her dancing that was almost incredible, especially for someone so young. Her quality of movement was so sharply hewn, and precise and strong, and not aggressive, but secure. And so I faced Grenier's kind of lyricism with her tautness, and that pleased me a lot because of the reversal. But I would say that is how the movement for those particular dancers came to be. It was in consideration of one to the other, back to back, and what had to pass between, to get from that one sort of movement of Bea's to Grenier's sort of movement. That was, then, the piece. Although I will say, I started in the middle, because originally, all I was going to do of the Haydn was the fourth movement because of the incredible energy and force. I mean just that blast that happens during the particular first and fourth finale; that was, as far as I knew, as much force coming out of music as anything I knew, and it was really exciting to me to challenge that visually, and to say, O.K., can I get that much flash? It's like a white glow, it's like something that is so hot that it almost disappears. And that's the kind of force it has. I started in the middle and worked out to both ends, after that section. Actually the sections weren't made this way in time, but they were made this way in my head. The fourth section was projected, and it didn't seem that it would be really long enough; somehow, it would make it difficult to program. So I said, we'll do the third movement before that; it will be a section of a more intimate nature, and it will be about people working together, and it will be made for soloists who are also capable of being ensemble workers. To me the most challenging area for really working at ideas is chamber music, and particularly the quartet. I think it is a form that has produced more real thinking than any other form at all, and this is because the members have to be capable of solo work, but have to go beyond that. They must not disregard that, but they have to take that for granted in a way, and concern themselves with something far, far more important. So that is what the second section became, and then out of that, I said to myself, well, I think I will abstract the whole piece, and present that first. Then that became the solo. And the solo was made last. And so on.

e.r. *I am impressed by your fascination with the architectural aspects of movement, and with the gut element of choreography.*

t.t. The movement, in particular for my company's work, evolves out of what the piece is. It was interesting to me making *As Time Goes By*, because it's really the first piece that I have made from another point of view, and in a way it was a much easier work for me to do because it already had a point of reference. It had the ballets that had been done, it had a whole tradition of ballet, it had a movement vocabulary, and what was called for was comment upon that which existed;

*Tied to a time when the United States as a cultural entity was still quite innocent. Twyla Tharp and members of her company in **The Bix Pieces** (Photo: Lois Greenfield)*

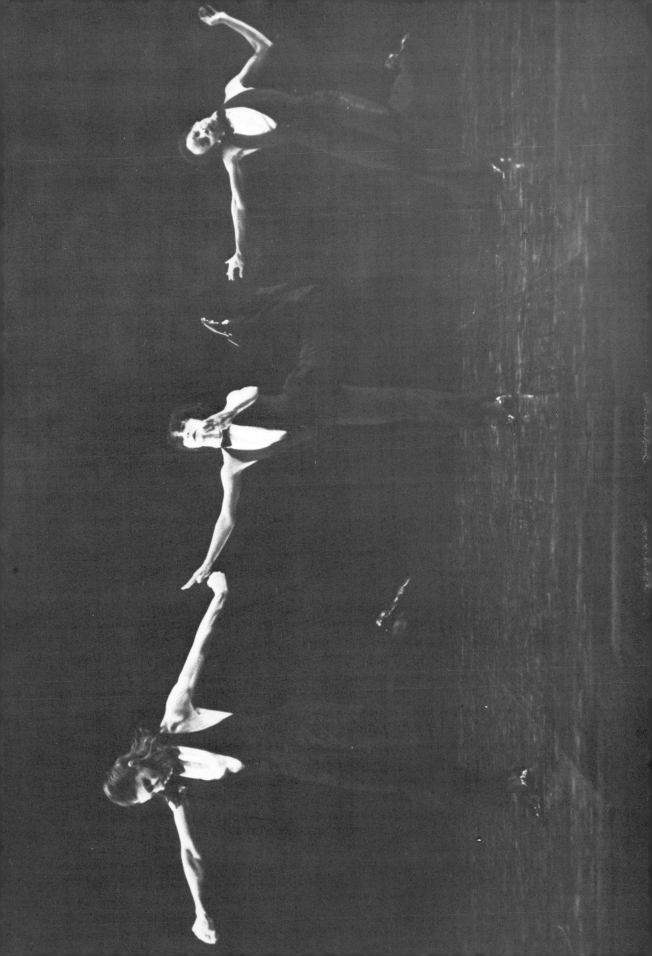

saying yes, I acknowledge this, yes, I challenge this, yes, I acknowledge this, but let us extend it. And to me, that was an enormous joy
and a relief from the—"terror" is almost the right word to use—of
attempting to have to define all those qualities from the beginning
each time we start a new piece of our own. I've always thought of
Agon, which I consider to be the classical ballet of the twentieth
century, in this way, because what Balanchine did was to assess the
point where ballet was, but then to say, all right, *but*. I mean, he said,
I can twist things in this way, I can literally twist the leg just a little bit
and make the audience see what they have become so habituated to
they can no longer see. And they will, in their mind, reconstruct the
old forms by my skewing it just a slight bit. That's a wonderful thing
to do, because it acknowledges the past, it acknowledges the tradition, and it makes it alive again. And that is the thing about classicism
that is always so moving to me. It acknowledges the past, but it also
revitalizes it. That's the difference between classicism which is something that is always an ongoing process, and neoclassicism, which is
something that is dead-ended and has no direction. I think that is a big
confusion that a lot of people have, the differentiation between
classicism and neoclassicism.

e.r. *That interests you, I mean, the fact of whether something is defined*
      as classicism.

t.t. It's all that concerns me.

e.r. *Why? Is it an intellectual kind of thing? Or is it just one of those*
      things that concerns you, and you don't even know why.

t.t. It's wanting to deal with something that is enduring, that has value.
      It's not wanting to buy a really cheap chair, it's wanting to buy a
      really good chair, and to use that really good chair every day instead
      of a really cheap chair. It's having something as total as it can be,
      which something that can be dispensed with tomorrow, that can be
      tossed out like a worn handkerchief, simply is not. I want something
      substantial, something of substance.

e.r. *Classical ballet is part of the tradition that started with the court*
      ballets, and I think it's easy to forget those original aristocratic roots.
      It just occurred to me that some of the movement, and the theme of
      your ballet, Deuce Coupe, *reflects our contemporary social dance;*
      only what a difference between today's loose, hip-rolling style, and
      the constrained elegance of the eighteenth- and nineteenth-century
      French courts. But, of course, the ballet, as well as the social dances,
      have passed through so many innovations, and in the future there will
      be other changes. That was one reason I asked you about your back-
      ground. I wasn't sure when you studied the classical ballet, or how
      you came to it, because there was a time when there were clear

compartments between the worlds of modern dance and of classical ballet. I think you've pulled some of the technical strands together. With your rippling type of movement, it's easy to forget there is a form underneath, because it looks so quick, and uncentered; it looks like ballet at moments, and like modern dance, as well.

t.t. Apparently it's confusing to some people. I like to think that the ballet is an enormously complete discipline. When I work within it, or outside it, either way, I'm always thinking about what is established there; what is available. Is it valid, or how is it not valid, right at this time. I ask myself where further can it go, rather than saying, "I don't need this." I'm going through it, by maintaining parts of it, by expanding other parts of it, and by discarding that which is just not sensible. I don't say in the beginning that I'm going to do away with ballet tradition, because that is foolish, because there is so much there. It cannot be discarded. For example, what you're saying about rippling through the body: in the ballet there is something, *épaulement*, which is badly understood by most ballet dancers, because it's badly taught, and too much is made of feet and legs, and too little of the shouldering, which is what *épaulement* means, and the *port de bras*, the carriage of the arms, off the shouldering. I heard a lot of flack about jazz movement in *As Time Goes By*: it's not jazz movement. The movement that I'm using is a condensed *épaulement*. It is an epaulement that has been abbreviated sometimes, that has been enlarged sometimes, but is still built, simply, by a torque around the spine. If one can look at something conceptually, and say *épaulement* is torque around the spine, it gives you a lot more freedom than if you simply say *épaulement* is *écarte*, is *éffacé*, and that's all it is. That is neoclassicism, to say that *épaulement* can only be the eight directions, but if you say, no, it is the torquing around the spine, then that gives you infinite possibilities, none of which contradict or threaten the ballet.

e.r. *You're talking, then, about the source, rather than the rigidity.*

t.t. Which is why I get so angry when people deny classicism to that ballet. There has been a lot of conjecture about the title, and *As Time Goes By* was named because it entertained me to use the title of a popular song that dealt in the notion of classicism, because "classical" is only defined as time goes by; that's the only way that one knows if something is classical or not. One will know if it endures, and if it continues to have content, and if it continues to have form; then it's classical. You cannot look at something, and say this is classical the minute it is done, because there are no standards other than time for defining classicism. So, I enjoyed taking a popular song title, which is supposed to dissipate itself, but has not. *As Time Goes By* remains a really beautiful song, and so does the movie. But classicism is a living thing.

e.r. *When you approach a work, do you usually work it out in your head, or do you work with the dancers, or do you make drawings?*

t.t. That depends entirely upon the piece. I used to make scripted works that were proposed in advance, and then simply executed. I did that, and that was a very Cunningham thing to do, because Merce used to propose, well, let us see what will arise if we suggest such and such, and so and so, and then this will come into being; it's not as though we thought of it in advance, and we'll have some lovely surprises. Yes, one does have some lovely surprises, but it's a very costly way, I have found, of getting to them. In other words, what I'm saying is that it is mostly not productive, although the few things that one might not have thought of in advance, but that do come up that way, can really be enormously valuable and educational, which is another thing. Sometimes, I try very hard to go into the studio with absolutely no notion, whatsoever, about what's going to be done, so that I am forced to look at exactly where things are that day. Exactly where is this dancer; what is this dancer up to at this very moment; instead of coming in with preconceived notions that say, Sara [Rudner] has been doing this well, so let's try this. It's seeing what Sara is about right this instant, and what that space is about this very instant; instead of knowing that the room has these particular dimensions, and the floor is irregular here, and it's irregular there, and so therefore we better do this here and that there; stopping and looking at it all over again. With *As Time Goes By*, there was a time pressure on that; it had to be finished within a certain period of time. The ballet was written in about five weeks, written and rehearsed in about five weeks. Therefore it was made with a lot of advance preparation. I used videotape quite a lot. I had the rehearsals videotaped, and then at home, I would look at the tape. I can save time that way, both in terms of rehearsing what has already been done, and in trying to figure out where it's going. Usually, the only strong idea that I have about a piece is a strong idea. I will want, very much, to make something of a certain sort, and that is usually what I go in with, and if that wanting is strong enough, something will come into being, and if it's not, then that work has to develop into something entirely different from what I thought it was going to be about in the beginning or it gets thrown out.

e.r. *So movement is really your speech. It's your way of communicating what you want to say.*

t.t. Not always, sometimes I also talk.

e.r. *Do you ever interchange the two, movement and speech on stage?*

t.t. Yes, in *The Bix Pieces*. There were certain things in *The Bix Pieces* that I did not feel could be said in movement, and therefore it was necessary to develop a text.

e.r. *What about the places where you work? Do you plan to work for a specific place; do you feel that the interaction between the audience and the place where the performers are dancing, influences the work?*

t.t.   Yes, that's very important to me. When I make a piece it's for specific dancers, and it's for a specific audience. For example, there's a piece of ours, called *The Fugue*, which was made for lecture-demonstrations in intimate spaces. *As Time Goes By* was made very much as a proscenium piece, knowing that some things, in some ways, are much more visible on a stage than they can be anywhere else. My first piece, called *Tank Dive*, was made for a small room in Hunter College that is actually a little auditorium on the sixteenth floor, and the whole piece is predicated for that space; I mean one of the walls curved, so a lot of the patterns had to do with that. It has very much to do with sight lines. It has to do with establishing what in that situation is visible; that's the core of all art. The work just comes out. But it is true, you try to define a situation according to what it can contain and what it has in it, and what is accessible through it. So something like *Medley*, which was made for an enormous outdoor space, acres and acres of property, was planned for what could be visible 300 yards away, and what could be visible right under your nose. Something like *Dancing in the Streets* was made to be done in a mob. It was to be done in an audience that was so deaf, because it was so large, that people would be dancing by, sort of poking around and trying to just get through; it was our subway dance. Let's see, architecture can also be considered. There's the proscenium stage, which I have come to find very beautiful. I found, by *not* working on proscenium stages, why proscenium stages were developed. There's a clarity and a control that you can exercise in a proscenium space. You simply cannot have the same effect if you are working in four different areas at one time. The proscenium space is the space most used for classical ballet, and that space, like the technique, can be treated in a vital way, or one can stay with a stultified use of both.

Twyla Tharp's own dance company is performing at the Brooklyn Academy of Music. A live orchestra has been brought in for this benefit evening, and it sits, dance-band style, behind the dancers on the large stage. An enthusiastic audience attentively watches the performance, charmed by the delightful mood and dancing of *The Bix Pieces*. Most of the music being played by the orchestra is a collection of Bix Beiderbecke's songs. Vaguely familiar, they are the sort of melodies that drifted through America's popular consciousness along with the popularity of Rudy Vallee records, and the big bands, which took the original jazz music and flattened it into a creamy, danceable music. Now, a trio of women dances dreamily around the stage to ''That's My Weakness Now.'' They are followed by an exhibition of double-handed baton-twirling from one of the dancers in a solo originally danced by Twyla; there are some lightly spoofed tap dancing and other miscellaneous bits and pieces of movement reflecting Twyla Tharp's nostalgic look back at an American girlhood.

For the second half of *The Bix Pieces*, Twyla Tharp, standing off center stage, away from the dancers and near the edge of the stage, recites her set narrative, "Why They Were Made." Her flat, no nonsense tone of voice has a refreshing nonchalance that is at odds with the slightly self-conscious text. "It seems to me that art is a question of emphasis. That aesthetics and ethics are the same. That inventiveness resides first in choice and then in synthesis." The dancing goes on, winding its way through Tharp's observations and comments about the technical and philosophical problems of making dances. Though the dance mirrors some of her own training and experience, the heart of *The Bix Pieces* is tied to a time when the United States as a cultural entity was still quite innocent. It was a period before Tharp's own birth, but she knows of it, and feels attached to it through her father, her culture, and the changes that came later. *The Bix Pieces* is the way Twyla Tharp has chosen to honor that era: ". . . the Twenties; before the Great Crash, when we still had time to be concerned with style."

Twyla Tharp is the evening's guest on Dick Cavett's TV talk show. Cavett has a dry witty style of speaking that matches Twyla's own, like the other half of a matching sweater set, but he is having little success in coaxing any small talk from his guest. After a while, he asks Twyla to teach him a "Tharp" dance. Everyone, it seems, has a secret inner desire to let loose and jiggle away. It's not quite as easy as it looks, as Cavett discovers when Twyla breaks apart a small pattern from one of her dances. As she gives him an on-the-spot lesson in the Tharp style of dancing, she becomes extremely professional in her attitude, and treats him as if he were a serious contender at a Tharp audition. In fact, Cavett gets a reprimand when he forgets the exact position of an arm placement. Cavett finds the whole process much more complex than he had expected, not realizing how Twyla places and sets each specific movement with an astonishing eye for detail. Cavett tries his best, but Twyla doesn't drop her reserve and smile until Dick brings out her young son, Jesse.

The daily papers carry a small item. Twyla Tharp has been engaged by Milos Forman to choreograph the dances and movement for his film version of the rock musical *Hair*. When the film is completed after a year's work, there are rumors that it has been heavily cut and that much of Twyla's work remains in the cutting room. Still, there is a heavy Tharp influence in the released version as the film keeps shifting in and out of the musical sequences she has choreographed.

When the opening shots of *Hair* zoom in to a group of hippies dancing about in Central Park, a close-up reveals Rose Marie Wright, a Tharp dancer of long standing. Some more close-ups and panning; is that Sara

Rudner, is that Twyla? I begin to have an odd feeling of watching a home movie during the dance sequences. There's a strangeness because the familiar faces have been pushed into the background of a false milieu. I think anyone acquainted with the Twyla Tharp Dance Company finds the juxtaposition of glamorous Hollywood and a group of nonglamorous modern dancers a little false. There's no mismatch of intention, as Twyla's work has the right flavor for this new kind of Hollywood musical film. It's a personal reaction. For anyone unfamiliar with the look of the Tharp dancers, their quirky movements and individual looks create a believable group of 1960's flower children, self-absorbed in doing their own thing. I really begin to wonder if it's playtime or another fantasy when Twyla, clothed in a cigarette-poster costume of an exotic priestess, appears in the wedding celebration dream sequence. Could Twyla and her company turn away from this Hollywood gamble, or is it one more challenge in the aesthetics of plotting dances? I'm not sure, and I don't know if it's fact or fantasy that best describes the moment when one becomes a movie star.

The "Dance in America" series televises Tharp's piece *Sue's Leg*, intercutting it with old film clips of social dances, marathon dancers, and other miscellaneous phenomena of the late 1920's and early 1930's. The period film clips, including one of Fats Waller playing the music Twyla Tharp uses for the ballet, flesh out her dances for the home audience by letting them see the generic, movement base of her work. With the counterpointing of images of real social dances and sections of *Sue's Leg*, there is an unusual opportunity to understand how Tharp feeds pieces of everyday gestures into her dances and then, like a jazz musician, plays with the movement. The main themes are reversed, slowed down, fractured apart, put together again, and it all happens so fast that everyone gets pulled along by the exuberance of the virtuosic dancing, losing sight of what's actually happening to the movement themes.

Tharp's choreography is extremely intricate, complex, and fast. She brilliantly uses the shifts of weight that support a dancer's movement and flow through the body in a walk, run, balance, leap, jump, and on to an infinity of possibilities. Weight shifts, and, in fact, any phrase of movement, is controlled by timing, which is one of the main keys to understanding the way Tharp manipulates movement phrases. And hers is a twentieth-century, American feeling of time, for things that are fast, shifting, and essentially rootless.

The ballet superstar, Mikhail Baryshnikov, tips the bowler hat sitting on his head, smiles to the audience, and with a mischevious shrug of a shoulder, opens the first few seconds of Twyla Tharp's ballet *Push Comes to Shove*. It's now 1976, and at Baryshnikov's request, Twyla has been commissioned by American Ballet Theatre to choreograph a ballet that will show him off. Baryshnikov's amazing technique makes him a perfect instrument for Twyla's demanding choreography. He responds brilliantly to her work, not only capturing Twyla's idiosyncratic style of movement in his dancing, but with a mimic's genius, recreating an exact image of Twyla Tharp. It's a tour de force of a ballet that ends speculation about Twyla's ability to choreograph in the classical style. Instead, it makes Twyla a "notorious" success and gives Baryshnikov an entirely new, but delightfully charming, role.

The Baryshnikov-Tharp partnership is so acclaimed that the two team up for a special benefit performance dancing a new Tharp work, *Once More Frank*. It's a once-only performance by the two dance celebrities in a dance about an American girl who grew up listening to the songs of Frank Sinatra, and a Russian boy who had a vague knowledge of the American life-style. For the girl, the playing of these songs involves a whole cultural mystique of growing up, finding romance, and living out the wistful melodies drifting through the familiar songs. For the boy, it is like touring another country. *Once More Frank* is a lesser venture into Tharp's own choreographic lodestone, but it gives Baryshnikov one more American experience.

As 1980 approaches, Twyla Tharp feels she is in a transitional period of her choreographic development. She has moved away from the concerns of our WBAI conversation which focused on the relationship between her work and the principles of classical ballet. Since *As Time Goes By*, her second ballet for the Joffrey Company, she has more than proven her originality and her talent as a ballet choreographer. In fact, Twyla Tharp has become an enormously popular success and her work is appreciated on its own terms.

Since the beginning of her career, Twyla Tharp has been willing to make changes in her choreographic efforts and to keep on growing in unexpected, unpredictable directions. Her choices have led her into a continuous exploration of dance form and content. Recently, she has used a touch of literal storytelling in dances taken from her work in *Hair*, and in *Chapters and Verses*, a work in progress. Another 1979 piece, *Baker's Dozen*, touches on autobiographical material by projecting film clips of her own pregnancy. Until this piece, Tharp's visual effects were achieved through good lighting and smartly designed costumes. In the future, she might further explore collaboration with visual artists, or she might further venture into dramatic storytelling.

It is doubtful that Twyla Tharp will remain the same, fitting the mold of her current popularity until the freshness fades and the fashionable audiences go elsewhere. What happens next must somehow relate to the overall direction and purpose of her work. I can't guess what will come out of her transitional period, but the question, quite clearly, is: What next, Twyla?

Meeting John Clifford

I'm rather brash, I suppose.

WHENEVER I USED TO SEE JOHN CLIFFORD in those clean, distilled, Balanchine ballets of the New York City Ballet Company, I thought of an airborne stream of floating bubbles. With his curly hair, dark brown eyes, and impish grin, Clifford appeared to be Puck's own image as he came flying out from the wings in performance after performance of the City Ballet. For even when his actual movements were relatively still, I had the feeling that he was holding down an irrepressible urge to leap about the stage.

Since there is always a thin line between a dancer's own personality and that of a choreographed role, it is often hard to separate the performer from the choreography. Though this is particularly true of nonstory, "abstract" ballets, it is also evident in a traditional story ballet where the character of the role either fits the natural quality of a dancer, or tests the dancer's acting skill. As the hoop-jumping leader of the candy canes in George Balanchine's version of *The Nutcracker*, Clifford perhaps comes closest to expressing the essence of his own nature through a dance role. The movements of the bright red-and-white-striped candy cane character and Clifford's temperament seem to be a perfect match of dance and dancer. When Jerome Robbins choreographed a frenetic solo for Clifford in *Dances at a Gathering*, he suggested that there might be a restless, churning intensity underlying all that excessive energy. It might be that Clifford's playful bounce is more complex than the enormous charm evident in a role like the sparkling candy cane. Whatever the source of Clifford's exuberance, or whatever roles make use of it, both Balanchine and Robbins, as well as the audience, know that the projection of this taut verve sets Clifford apart from the other dancers and gives him a distinct dancing personality.

Since Clifford's choreographic personality is now developing, the question that comes first to my mind is whether Clifford's choreography will reflect the same quality of energy as his dancing. But only time and future ballets can answer that. Nerve he must have, however, for it takes a lot of confidence to experiment with your own choreography while working under the direct, watchful eyes of the formidable George Balanchine. Not only is the Russian-born Balanchine (or as everyone associated with the New York City Ballet Company calls him, "Mr. B.") the artistic force that shaped the company, he is the poet of twentieth-century ballet. In addition, Jerome Robbins, the second choreographer of the company, is a man whose plentiful talent ranks him as America's finest ballet choreographer. A hopeful young choreographer like Clifford must subject his work to the critical eyes of these two men before it can be presented on stage, to be danced by the New York City Ballet.

When the ballet is finally scheduled, the fledgling choreographer still faces the reactions of both a press and an audience spoiled by a repertoire of ballets by Balanchine and Robbins. It might just take all that reserve of energy that John Clifford has displayed in his dancing to face the task of pushing his own choreography through some very tough barriers.

I find that with all my liking for John Clifford the dancer, I am not an innocent member of the audience when it comes to appraising his choreographic efforts. I appreciate his problems as a new choreographer, but looking at my performance notes for 1969–1970, I see that I thought his *Sarabande and Dance* "interesting" (whatever that meant), and *Reveries* "slower-paced than a Balanchine piece and missing those gasps that a Robbins work always creates." Annoyed by my own hubris, I decide to include John Clifford in the choreographers series so that he, personally, could say what gives him the courage to show his developing choreographic skills in the midst of such a blazing atmosphere of perfected excellence.

e.r. *I feel now, talking to you, as though I'm speaking to someone I know even though we are meeting for the first time. I've seen you on stage so many times that I think I know you. I always enjoy watching you dance.*

j.c. You know me, if you've seen me.

e.r. *Seen you dance?*

j.c. Sure.

e.r. *I saw* The Symphony in E, *the work you did for the Stravinsky Festival.*

j.c. My "Ken Russell" ballet? No one understood it, but that's all right. The Symphony in E was Stravinsky's first symphony, and he was very influenced by every other composer at that time, especially his teacher, Rimsky-Korsakov. Also, the whole third movement is basically Tchaikovsky's Sixth Symphony; also, there's a lot of Wagner, and the first movement is Richard Strauss. As a matter of fact, every time Balanchine walked in or heard the music, he said, "All that Strauss, that Strauss," and I said, "You know who it is." Balanchine made the piano reduction for me [the piano version of the orchestrated score], which is very nice, but a little frightening since it means

Puck's own image. John Clifford (Courtesy of the Los Angeles Ballet Company)

that he knows every single note in that symphony, and naturally, it's not what he would have done to it.

Mr. B. requested that I use Gelsey Kirkland and Peter Martins for all four movements of the ballet, which really gave me a bit of a handicap because no ballet has one set of principals for that long. The ballet was almost forty minutes long, so I had to think of some idea and I put exaggerations in the ballet because it's a very youthful piece. It's almost a cliché-sounding symphony. If you really listen to it, it's not Stravinsky, it's very clichéd, and old, lush romanticism. I did a little take-off on romantic ballet to match it.

e.r.   *How do the mechanics go for putting on a ballet here with the New York City Ballet?*

j.c.   It's always different. Just before Jerry Robbins became associated with the company again, I was doing more, but now there's no time. Though I've done seven ballets. They come and go quickly, but I really don't want my ballets to settle into the repertoire because I agree completely with Mr. B. when he describes his ballets as being ephemeral works that come and go. A couple of my ballets have stayed a while; *Fantasies*, which is about three or four years old, is usually in every other repertoire, which means every other season. That's all right, but most of them I'm glad to do just as an experimental piece, and have them gone.

I'm young still, but I'm so tired of being young and promising, you know. I'm really not too paranoid about doing a "masterpiece." It was Mr. B., actually, who said something like "If you start off to do a masterpiece, how will you ever know when you've got it done?" It's a funny line. Otherwise, I think I'd become paranoid with all the masterpieces that are in this company.

I've accepted the fact that I'm a real Balanchine disciple, but I didn't want to be for a long time. I didn't want to be that chauvinistic about the company. Now, if anyone starts in on another choreographer, or the things wrong with this company, which I know there are, I just go crazy because I see the things that are right with this company and right with Mr. Balanchine. Now we have Jerry Robbins, the other great choreographer, I think, in the world.

e.r.   *Do you think that you're influenced by both people, or both ways of working?*

j.c.   Jerry I consider mainly a director. He won't like this, but he never does like anything I say. When he's choreographing his ballets, he doesn't like the audience to know exactly what the dramatic viewpoints in the ballet are, but he puts them in; it's just his way of working. I think it has to do with his having been with Ballet Theatre, which is a very programmatic company, especially compared to ours, and because of all those shows he did on Broadway. And so Jerry, even in ballets like *Dances at a Gathering* or *Goldberg Variations*, is used to having some kind of story in his ballets. I said this once in an interview in *Ballet Review* and he had a fit, but he didn't say anything to me.

e.r. *I don't know about a specific story as a plot, but I always feel that something is happening to the people in a Robbins ballet.*

j.c. It's pretty definite.

e.r. *Then it's more of a story?*

j.c. It's surprisingly definite what Jerry wants, but he doesn't want this let out to the audience. It would then ruin the idea of the audience making up its own stories, and that's what he really wants. And that's all right, that's just his way of working. Balanchine's way of working, for the most part, is so totally different. Whatever music Balanchine uses, the ballet is just another melodic line. Other critics have said it. It's really obvious that it's not *on* the music, it's not *with* the music, it has nothing to do with a story, it *takes* the music, and *writes* another melodic line or tempo or whatever, and sometimes, it's in total disagreement with the music. This really used to bother me until I got used to it. I didn't understand what they were doing. Now, it's terribly interesting.

In each performance of a Balanchine ballet, i can find something new. I suppose if I'm influenced by anyone, it is Balanchine. I'm trying in vain to understand how Balanchine does it. I know it's all his musical background and I haven't had it, and that's partially my fault. When I first came here, he tried to push me very hard into piano studies, which I had a little of, and I balked. I was very independent then. "I want to be this, and I want to do it my way, and blah, blah, blah." And it was very stupid of me.

e.r. *How old were you at the time? Seventeen?*

j.c. I was nineteen. I didn't come to New York until I was eighteen. Now I regret it all because the way Balanchine does it is simply because he's such a musician.

e.r. *Are you trying to do extra piano studies now?*

j.c. No, not really, but it's slowly becoming clearer. I don't want to pattern my choreography after him. I mean I don't want to become a carbon copy, but I do at least want to have some understanding of the way he works with music. And he's told me in very simple language, how, if music is complicated then the steps should be simple. He's said not to try to be right on the music; that I shouldn't do what I hear muscially, but I should do what's written in the score. In *Rubies*, for instance, Balanchine has everyone end one count later. He said, "It goes one, two, three, one, two, three, one, two, silence on three . . ." He wanted the dancers to go up in the air on the note and to land on the silence in unison. It's very difficult to get twenty-four dancers up in the air and then land, one count later, very quickly. At one performance of *Rubies* that I watched from out front, it really worked. Everyone went up and landed on the silence. It was so effective, it was frightening. Yet, Balanchine tossed it off. It's always better to watch all the dancers in a Balanchine ballet, rather than one particular one. If you're sitting up top, it's easier to watch the whole stage.

e.r.　*How did you start doing your own work in the company?*

j.c.　Mr. B. told me that whenever I felt like doing a ballet that I should keep pushing them out. He wanted me to do a lot of choreography while I had the interest and while I was very energetic. Usually, it would be a question of which ballet I had in mind. The most important thing was whether Mr. B. liked the music.

e.r.　*How do you usually start? Do you pick the music for the beginning step?*

j.c.　Always. Sometimes the music is programmatic, like the Vaughan Williams Fantasia. It took me a long time to think of what story I would do to that. And sometimes it's just obviously nonprogrammatic, to me anyway, so I don't worry about it. I just get to know the music and then go into the studio.

e.r.　*Do you decide how many dancers and which ones? I know that you handled something like thirty-two dancers for your ballet* Symphony in E. *That's a lot of people to work with and to tell what to do.*

j.c.　There were thirty-seven dancers in my first ballet for the company, a work to Stravinsky's Symphony in C. People said that I must be terribly conceited to use so many dancers in my first novice work for a major company. But *Symphony in C* evolved from a student workshop when I was at the School of American Ballet. Edward Villella was supposed to do a ballet for the spring season in '68, but he had other commitments, and my ballet was half done at the school. Mr. B. asked me if I could do it for the company. I said yes. I didn't come up to Mr. B. and say, "I have a major work . . ." He needed a ballet. That's the way this company usually works, which is nice because it's sort of businesslike. And the only reason that I used thirty-seven dancers was because it was a very big symphony. I'm very struck with that. I can't do a big symphony and have two people on stage.

e.r.　*What happens then? Do you look for particular dancers to express a special work or feeling?*

j.c.　Exactly.

e.r.　*Then do you go up to the dancers you want and tap them on the shoulder?*

j.c.　It's only courtesy to go up to principal dancers, ballerinas and *premier danseurs* and talk to them first, and say "I have an idea for a ballet and I'm probably going to do it in the spring, and I would like to use you." They always say yes, but it's just courtesy. It's rude to have their name down on the schedule and not even talk to them. As far as the corps de ballet goes, you just call whomever you need, when you need them.

e.r. *Do you change things when you start to work with the dancers or do you have it all set in your head beforehand?*

j.c. No. I don't know any choreographer that does that, except, maybe Jerry. He pretty much knows what he wants to do. Mr. B. knows the music, but he really doesn't know anything when he comes into the room; it's incredible. As you see, I like to talk about Balanchine. With the *Symphony in E* piece that I did for the Stravinsky Festival, Mr. B. suggested Peter Martins and Gelsey Kirkland because, as you know, we did about twenty new ballets that one week. Mr. B. didn't want all the dancers to be used in every ballet. At that point, anyway, Peter and Gelsey weren't really too involved in anything. I said fine, and Peter was most helpful when he danced. He did everything full out all the time. I was surprised because he's European and classical in demeanor. Mr. B. told me, "Teach him how to move, teach him how to move fast." Peter was used to *Swan Lake* and to *Giselle*, and here in our company, we use a different approach to the technique. I think Peter has changed tremendously and he's more comfortable in our ballets. I've never had any trouble with any of the dancers I've worked with before this, but Gelsey gave me quite a lot of trouble.

It was really odd because Peter was so willing to do anything, even if he felt awkward in it; even if I asked him to stand on his head. He really wanted to do whatever the choreographer said and not worry if he felt wrong in it because he was learning through Mr. B. that he could look even better on stage. But Gelsey was going through the phase of trying not to be a young girl, but to be a mature ballerina. She had a lot of responsibilities on her shoulders and she was very young to be a ballerina. Gelsey does have the potential to be a classical ballerina—whatever that is—but she was getting pressure from a lot of people to be "classical" so she started thinking that this company wasn't classical, which was a mistake, and I think she's learning. But she did give me trouble; she wouldn't do anything I asked for in rehearsal. I was very upset because I'm not the most secure person in the world, anyway, and Peter was being very helpful, the corps de ballet kids were tired because we were working on a lot of things and I couldn't push them too hard because they had so many other rehearsals. I had to have some thought for them and Gelsey, who was not rehearsing anything else at that time, wouldn't do anything. She didn't understand how I wanted the last movement. I explained it to her, but she didn't believe that I wanted the last movement to be a great big, schmaltzy Bolshoi, Russian, Petipa, polonaise finale.

We didn't have any ballets in the whole Stravinsky week that had that kind of Stravinsky music and we weren't going to have any sort of classical ballets like that. I mean ballets that were so big. I wanted this ballet to be very different. I had a very difficult time trying to get Gelsey to dance flashy enough for the end. I wanted her to look like a ballerina, which she wanted, but then at that point she was also going through a subtle stage. Gelsey wanted everything to be subtle. I was very, very upset or otherwise I wouldn't be saying this. Finally, I told Gelsey, "If you don't want to dance it, you go in [to Balanchine] and say something, but I'm certainly not going to do anything." So she danced very well. Gelsey always dances well when she wants to. In Saratoga, I taught it to Merrill Ashley, who picked it up immediately and everything went well because I could change things that I didn't like that Gelsey was doing. And now I'm happy because everyone was surprised by Merrill's performance. The best thing about being a choreographer, really, aside from having a ballet work, when it does, is to see young dancers go out there and do something incredible. Merrill even frightened me because I didn't know that she could do it like that. Balanchine was pleased, Robbins was pleased, everyone was pleased, and that made me happy. For me to see her flower like that was worth doing the whole ballet.

e.r.   *That's a part of the way you work then—becoming involved with the dancers that you use?*

j.c.   Not all choreographers do, but when I'm working with a dancer, I inevitably take them out for dinner or have coffee with them. If you don't like someone, no matter how good a dancer they are, it's very difficult to work with them.

    There are so many dancers in this company that we all have learned that no one is indispensable. When Merrill stood in for Gelsey, she surprised everyone because it's a technically difficult role. Gelsey is a strong technician, so consequently when you work with a strong dancer, you start giving them things they can do or something they can look good in. I didn't change the tricks for Merrill and she did them all.

e.r.   *Back to some of the mechanics.*

j.c.   Mechanics, O.K. You find the music and you find the dancers with the personalities or technique that you want or that will suit the music. If it's a programmatic score, then you find dancers who are rather warmer than, say, other dancers.

e.r.   *Then it's a quality in the dancer that you're looking for.*

j.c.   I think all choreographers and artists work that way. Then I clear it with Balanchine because he's the boss. I've had my situations where

"You take the music and you get ideas." The Los Angeles Ballet in Clifford's Symphony *(Courtesy of the Los Angeles Ballet Company)*

he doesn't agree with me, and I've not gone over his head because you can't. I sort of press, though, and he says, "All right, try it." One of those was *Fantasies*, and that was the most successful ballet I've had here. And then there are other ballets, where he says, "Oh, this music is fabulous, do it." That happened with Stravinsky's Symphony in C which turned into a big disaster because I really, really didn't want to do the music that much. So it works both ways. Some ballets that I've tossed out, like *Sarabande and Dance*, stayed in the repertoire. I was the one who got it canceled. I didn't want it to go anymore.

e.r. *It was lovely.*

j.c. I didn't know.

e.r. *How do you actually work out the steps?*

j.c. On the dancers. I don't do anything by myself.

e.r. *You know the music very well when you go in and then it sort of comes? Do you rely on the dancers to remember?*

j.c. They always do. That's a dancer's job.

e.r. *And what about you, do you remember from day to day or do you write notation?*

j.c. No, I never take any notes. It's not hard to remember at all. You become so used to remembering, especially if you're with Balanchine's company. You know so many steps, so many counts. I wouldn't be a bit wrong, I think, for saying that the dancers in this company have better memories, or quicker, faster minds than dancers in most other companies. We proved it during the Stravinsky Festival week. What other company could have done twenty new ballets in one week? Some of the corps dancers were in eight or nine new ballets, and that meant two new ballets a night. They all remembered everything; no one made any mistakes, and it was at the end of a very long season. They were proud of their work.

e.r. *There was a lot to be proud of, but aside from Mr. Balanchine, who I see is a big influence in your life . . .*

j.c. I have to say Balanchine because the way he works is the way I work. And you can't learn choreography. I try and work the way Balanchine works. The only way I've learned anything about choreography is by watching him work, or watching Jerry work. How do you define choreography? You take the music and you get ideas. Sometimes something comes out of an accident. Dancers trip over each other and it looks good, and I say "Keep it." Or sometimes I think something is going to work and I go in there, and I say "I'm going to have these ten girls do all this," and it's a disaster.

e.r. *What is your background in dance? Where were you before you came to the New York City Ballet Company?*

j.c. I was a Hollywood actor. Ready?

e.r.   *A child actor?*

j.c.   Yes. My parents were in show business. My mother was a singer and my father was an acrobat. I was in my father's act when I was, like, three.

e.r.   *You actually grew up on the stage.*

j.c.   Born in a trunk and all that. I studied tap and jazz and ballet. Then I met Mia Plisetskaya [in Los Angeles] and studied with the Bolshoi when I was eighteen. I hadn't really felt that I was going to be a classical ballet dancer until then. I knew I had to choreograph, but I wasn't really sure if I wanted to choreograph ballets. I did my first choreography for a stock company production of *West Side Story* in Los Angeles when I was fifteen. I don't think Jerry knew about it.

e.r.   *You were fifteen?*

j.c.   Originally, I was supposed to play Baby John. They were going to use the Jerome Robbins choreography if they could get permission, which is very difficult. I had choreographed a solo for myself to audition with and the director said, "Who did that number for you?" And I said, "I did." And he said, "Oh, that's very interesting." And I said, "Why, do you need a choreographer?" I'm rather brash, I suppose. I'm tired of fighting that image. If I am, I am.

e.r.   *When you set out to do a piece, or a ballet, and you've got the dancers on the stage, and you've got the people in the audience, do you ever think in terms of what it is you'd like the people in the audience to respond to? Do you want to thrill them by putting a lot of versatile acrobatics on stage?*

j.c.   It depends on the music. Every now and then I have music I have to do. I listen to music a lot. It ruins my sleep, but I love music very much. And I like this company because it's so musical. Some people say that I'm too musical. Jerry Robbins gets very mad at me. He says he doesn't like it because I accentuate the music. That makes me really want to tear my hair out because I can't help it. I don't do it on purpose; but, there's this crash somewhere and I have a step that goes crash, and I can't help it if they crash at the same time. When Mr. B. has choreographed ballets for me, like *Danse Concertante* and *Waltz Fantasy*, he knows what I'm going to do. Mr. B. will throw something at me and he knows I'm going to crash there, so he doesn't even tell me. Then afterwards I may ask him, "Is this wrong?" and he'll say, "No." So, consequently I try and do the same things. When I use people for certain qualities, I don't try and tell them to do anything. I let them do what they're going to do anyway.

e.r.   *You don't work against their grain?*

j.c.   You can pull a dancer a bit and you can try and make them expand their natural abilities, but I think it's ridiculous to try and make some dancer into what he or she isn't. If you want a different quality, there's a different dancer. If you want someone who is going to be very chic and musical, there's Violette Verdy. Then if you want a dancer to be terribly dramatic and intensely flingy, there's Sara Leland. And Kay Mazzo is always going to have a calm quality. Gelsey Kirkland is going to be securely on balance and a great technician; you don't have to worry about anything you hand her. Merrill Ashley, I think, is one of our most cleanly pure classical dancers coming up in the company. Eddy Villella is a jumper, Helgi Tommasson is a technician, Jacques d'Amboise is personality for days. I mean everyone has a different quality.

e.r. *I think you found a good home that will keep you busy for a long time to come.*

j.c. There are problems. As you said in the beginning, working under Mr. B. isn't easy. He doesn't do anything on purpose, but it does make me feel terribly inadequate before I start. I know I'm in a learning experience here at the New York City Ballet. I go into a room and begin to choreograph, and I sort of think why bother—because Balanchine's done everything that I would like to do. But I think that maybe there'll be something I can do at some later time. And I'm still such an active dancer that when I do choreograph, I'm very aware of how a dancer feels. So, the problems are very small compared to all the things I'm learning. I'm not pushing to make any great dent in the choreographic world right now. I'm dancing a lot; I'm trying to do some good ballets. One thing I'm trying to do is to make each ballet a little different. It's okay if people want to read things into my ballets; or if they think it's a Balanchine steal, then if it's a good one, that's all right. I'm glad I have some reputation. I don't know if I've deserved it, but I try to work hard at what I'm doing.

1979

e.r. *When did you leave the New York City Ballet Company and become the artistic director of the Los Angeles Ballet Company?*

j.c. In March of '73 I received a call from the Los Angeles Junior Ballet, the local regional company, asking if I'd do a ballet for them. Initially, I said, "No." However, a few friends of mine—Allegra Kent, Sara Leland, and Brian Pitts [New York City Ballet dancers]—were interested in the possibility of doing a concert out in Los Angeles during the lay-off period. Since I went home to Los Angeles during that time anyway, I called back and said, "If you can set up a few performances for my friends, then I'll do a ballet and we'll all guest." That worked out well, and the Los Angeles Times did an article about me. Some businesspeople saw the piece and contacted me about coming out full-time to start a company. At first I said, no, I'd come out only on my vacation periods. I did that until the spring of '74, when I decided that I should make a total commitment to help get the Los Angeles company off the ground.

e.r. *To leave the New York City Ballet and become the director/ choreographer for a nascent company is an enormous change. It's also a lot of responsibility.*

j.c. I talked about going out there with Mr. B [George Balanchine], and he was very helpful. He said that if it didn't work out, I could come back to City Ballet. In essence, I see the job of artistic director as that of a teacher and a ballet master. I'd been teaching at the School of American Ballet since I was twenty-one and I'd also done a lot of choreography, including eight ballets for City Ballet, so the job didn't seem formidable to me. In fact, I was at a point in my own choreographic maturation where, for better or worse, I had to get away and be on my own. Also, I was beginning to feel guilty for training the dancers in Los Angeles and then leaving them there without me.

e.r. *And the dancers that you were using were trained by your ex-teacher, Irena Kousnovska?*

j.c. In the very beginning, yes. Irena has always had a reputation for turning out incredible dancers. Then, when I moved back to Los Angeles in July of 1974, Johnna Kirkland, a soloist in the New York City Ballet, came with me. Nancy Davis, a soloist in the National Ballet in Washington, was out in Los Angeles at that time, and so she joined right away. A few other City Ballet dancers who were originally from Los Angeles decided to join our company. But the majority of the corps were Irena's advanced students who came when they could. There weren't many boys in the beginning, but we now have twenty-seven dancers and a forty-week contract. It has taken us awhile, but we average about one hundred performances a year. It's worth doing.

e.r. *Don't you do a special summer festival as well?*

j.c. For the last two years, the Los Angeles County Music and Performing Arts Divison has funded us very generously in a series of outdoor performances that are free to the public. We're packed and the County pays for most of it. We also perform at the Greek Theatre for a week, usually in conjunction with a pop group. This year we'll be the opening act for George Benson. It compromises me, but I have to make ends meet. I have to give the dancers their salaries . . . and it's kind of fun.

e.r. *What else is on your company's schedule?*

j.c. We're excited because we finally got the momentum to do a *Nutcracker* at the Music Center this year. I'm going to follow the original Petipa [Marius Petipa, original choreographer of *The Nutcracker*] libretto and notes which are very similar to Mr. B.'s version. There's a lot of humor in it and a lot of special effects. We've found all the notes that Petipa wrote to Tchaikovsky during the composition of the piece.

e.r. *Where did you find the notes?*

j.c. Our music director is really an academician, and he found them in the Tchaikovsky Collection at the University of California at Los Angeles. We found an English dance that's about two minutes long and was originally supposed to be in the second act. We're going to put it in, so it'll be the world premiere of that bit of music, and we're happy about that. After *The Nutcracker*, I'm doing the three-act *Sylvia* for 1981. I think big ballets are coming back in.

e.r. *I've never seen it. What's it about?*

j.c. This will be the first American production and I'll follow the original plot which is charming, funny, and almost camp. Sylvia is a nymph/goddess. A shepherd falls in love with her and she thinks he presumes too much, so she shoots him. Then the statue of Eros comes alive and shoots her with a love arrow. There's also a comic figure, Orion, a hunter, who kidnaps Sylvia. In act two, Sylvia is in his lair, and she gets him drunk on wine. Eros comes and helps her escape . . .

e.r. *Are you going to do it straight?*

j.c. Yes, but it can't be done absolutely straight with today's standards. We'll do it in knee length tulle costumes, and leopard skins, and golden bows. It'll be great fun. The best thing about *Sylvia* is the music. Stravinsky was right when he said Delibes was the greatest ballet composer. Mr. B. has said the same, and the music is very, very dancey and luscious. I'm really looking forward to working on it.

e.r. *I understand that you choreographed some twenty new ballets in the first year of the Los Angeles Ballet Company's existence.*

j.c. The dancers had to have something to dance. At first, Balanchine supplied the ballets and I choreographed the bread-and-butter fare. Mr. B.'s generosity is just incredible. He doesn't charge anything for his ballets. We only paid for the ballet mistress to stage them. Also, we had to build a whole new audience for ballet in Los Angeles because our style was unfamiliar. It's an educational process. I've been building an audience of younger people who come to the ballet to see dancing instead of expecting the traditional *Swan Lake*. In the first years, I veered more towards commercial things. I did a Scott Joplin ballet and a work to a Ravi Shankar sitar concerto. One ballet we did caused a bit of scandal because it had some nudity. A little scandal is good every now and then.

e.r. *Especially if you want attention for your company.*

j.c. I didn't do it for that reason only. The piece had to have some nudity in it, but of course everyone thought I was doing it only for the scandal. Lately I haven't choreographed that much for the company. One reason I did so many ballets in the first few years was that I had some very, very fine dancers who weren't being paid well. They had to get something out of it, so consequently I choreographed for them. Even though no one ever came and said anything, I could tell when they needed a little something to perk them up. Also, we had forty-eight weeks of work and I had to keep everyone busy. Most of it was craft, but then every once in a while, I'd do something like *Transcendental Études* that I just had to do. The music just knocked me out. I had to choreograph it. It's an hour and twenty minutes of Franz Liszt's piano music, but I had to do it.

e.r.   *Your range of music is extensive; you've used scores by Bartók, Fauré, Saint-Saëns, Stravinsky, Albinoni, Liszt, and others. Do you listen to music all the time? How do you find what you want?*

j.c.   I listen to music all the time, and I have the help of my musical director, Dr. Clyde Allen. I like different kinds of music, and I want to give the kids in the company a variety of things to dance. You can't just take class if you're in a company, and you can't keep rehearsing the same repertoire or you'd go crazy. But, again, I have to be pragmatic. It depends on the house we're going into and what the minimum is. I had ten chamber ballets one season simply because the house we were going into wouldn't let us use tape. We perform with a live orchestra only occasionally, and usually it's a chamber orchestra.

e.r.   *Your feeling for choreography seems to develop from the music.*

j.c.   The music is the beginning. If there's a story or if there's a plot that I want to do, then I'd rather have the music composed for it. There are few things that I'm a stickler on, and one of them is using scores. I hate it when somebody takes a score that was written for a particular ballet and then does a completely different story to it. That I don't like at all. I've seen all sorts of versions of *Firebird* that had nothing to do with the original ballet based on the Russian fairy tale. Stravinsky wrote the music for a particular story and it's rude to him when the score is used for another purpose. I can be accused of not being musical, myself. I took a huge Saint-Saëns organ symphony and made a huge ballet to it, but I didn't put on a story to it.

e.r.   *You just used the essence of the music?*

j.c.   I find it hard to do story ballets . . .

e.r.   *Because it doesn't interest you at this point?*

j.c.   I like to be dramatic. Two years ago I did a Debussy ballet to Les Images, Books One and Two. I didn't really put a story onto it, but it has emotions in it. That I like to do, but that's as far as I want to superimpose things.

e.r.   *After the music is chosen, do you plot out the steps?*

j.c.   I haven't done just steps in years. If you have an emotion or joy or sadness, or whatever, you want to get that emotion out of the material. Thinking of steps alone doesn't do it.

e.r.   *You mean putting together a series of steps like an enchainment?*

j.c. Yes, there's got to be a reason. Mr. B. always used to say to me, "Steps, boring." Anybody can do steps. The trick is to make something special out of them. Mr. B. is so fine a musician that the way his steps and the music interlock is extraordinary; but that's unique. Everybody imitates his approach of using music because the way he does it so interesting. It's not done on purpose and there's nothing wrong with it, but there's only one Balanchine. The results don't come out looking the same as Mr. B.'s work even though the method seems to be the same, and it's frustrating. That is one of the reasons that I left City Ballet, because I was guilty of that myself. I saw it coming, and I said, "If I want to choreograph, I'd better really do something of my own."

e.r. *Do you find you're now working in a different way?*

j.c. I can't take a really objective look at my own choreography.

e.r. *I don't mean the end result, I mean the process, your way of working.*

j.c. Not much change. The eight early ballets that I did for City Ballet were really an apprenticeship period for me. Some of the ballets turned out well, and some of them didn't turn out so well. I think I was lucky that as many turned out as well as they did. In those days, Mr. B. impressed upon me that choreography is a craft as much as anything else. He would always compare turning out ballets to making furniture. Choreography is an art, possibly. You're inspired once in a while, but if you're the director of the company, or the ballet master, then you've got to be a craftsman.

When I started with the Los Angeles company, I had to do a lot of furniture making, but every now and then, there's been a piece of music, like the Liszt Études, that I've had to do. Those *Transcendental Études* kept me up at night. If I can't sleep, I know I have to choreograph the music. It only happens about once every other year. This time it was an absolute nightmare. I sat outside and drove everyone crazy playing this Liszt piano music, over, and over, and over again. I couldn't hear just one section the first time I heard those études, I had to hear the whole work, and it's long. I put the record on and sat with a glass of wine in my hand. I was crying by the end of it. Deep down I'm a mushy person. Some of the kids didn't like the music when they heard it at first, but I said, "You'll get used to it." Now they love it.

e.r. *You had the music in your blood when you started to work with the dancers.*

j.c. It's really like a disease. The kids know when I've got to get a piece of music out of my system. I see this look going across their faces. "Oh, this is going to be a hard day." For better or for worse, I did an hour-and-a-half worth of piano music in about ten days of frantic choreographing. It's pretty heavy, but there are some moments that I'm proud of.

e.r. *Do you still work it out as you go?*

j.c. I don't have anything set. I know what section I'll be doing and who's dancing what.

e.r. *You know the music . . .*

j.c. I know the music. I don't come in unless I know what I'm doing musically. I choreograph very fast. Some people will say you can't work as fast as I do. They say, ''Maybe if you tried to work slower, it might even be better . . .'' I've asked them to guess which ballets I've done fast and which ones I've done slowly, and invariably they pick the ones that I've choreographed quickly as their favorites. With the Liszt, I really raced. I was going all day long, from right after class in the morning until about six at night. My dancers know when I'm going like that they better remember it the next day or it's hopeless. They do, though, and I'm proud of them because they're so smart.

e.r. *Do you remember what you've done?*

j.c. I remember most of it. I don't change things either, unless something is terrible, and then I change it later. Again, it's the training. As a dancer, I did many ballets with Mr. B., and I learned to do the job and to remember. There are two ways of approaching this work; one is to consider it a job involving a craft, the other is to approach it as an ''artiste.'' I say the hell with that. When I work, I can't be involved with sturm and drang and all that sort of emoting. I do all that at home, at night, when I'm listening to music.

A rehearsal for what John Clifford calls ''the popular side'' of the Los Angeles Ballet is scheduled for this Tuesday morning, immediately after the morning's class. The dancers, Johnna Kirkland, Laura Flagg, Dana Lynn Shwarts, Richard Fritz, James Lane, and Brian Pitts start working on a series of pas de deux to the music of George Benson, the popular jazz/ballad singer. Pleased with this section of the work, Clifford starts to set the last song, which uses all six dancers. Dressed casually, in sneakers and corduroy jeans, he sits down with his back to the mirrored wall and carefully observes his small group rehearse to the taped music. From time to time he gets up to demonstrate a particular movement, or as now, in order to clarify a difficult, swooping lift in which the girls are swung over their partner's heads, rest on a shoulder, and then land in a fish dive. ''Brian, lift Laura and turn the way James just did,'' suggests Clifford. They try it. ''No, not exactly . . .'' he says and motions with his arms. Johnna demonstrates, Clifford nods in approval, takes a sip from the bottle of diet soda in his hand, sits down, and the dancers start again, from the beginning.

It's the day before the opening night performance of the company's five-day stint as part of George Benson's concert at the Greek Theatre, an open air amphitheatre that seats 4,500 people and is already sold out to the Benson fans. The Los Angeles Ballet is working with the Benson group for the first time today, and around one P.M. someone starts bringing in the colorful, metal boxes that hold the jazz group's electric instruments. The musicians, including George Benson, arrive a short time after. They settle in and the rehearsal starts. The musicians start playing, but the dancers can't begin dancing as they aren't able to figure out their opening measure. Benson comments, "Someone spliced the tape and we're going to be a measure short if we follow through that way." Johnna and Clifford do some more explaining; Benson watches the group dance out the section with the tape, and then says simply to his group, "Play in measures." That helps because the dancers correlate their movements and the music through counts, in this instance, a measure of one two three four, two two three four . . . The musicians start again. This time they hold their rhythm to a measure, the dancers find their place in the music, and the rehearsal is on its way.

There is no such thing as a lunch break for the dancers who have been dancing since their early morning class. Instead, they take a cup of coffee, nibble on chocolate, or pick up a snack from a canteen van that periodically arrives outside in the alley between the studio and the neighboring garage. Clifford continues to take sips from his bottle of soda throughout the afternoon, and remains soft-spoken, alert, and good humored, even though the musicians and the dancers must rehearse one section again and again and again, trying to iron out a timing problem.

In *Benson Songs*, the piece everyone is working on, Clifford has taken the mood of each of the songs and run a choreographic study relating to it, rather than interpreting the strong rhythmic jazz beat. Some of the resulting choreography is slick, but there are also sections that are pure and subtle. Clifford has a way with startling, beautiful lifts that emerge out of nowhere and quickly shift into other lifts, other patterns. Still, this particular combination of music and movement is like oil and water; it just doesn't mix well.

John Clifford has been working like this over the last six years, giving his heart, his head, and his energy to the Los Angeles Ballet, a young company of spirited dancers. That irrepressible Clifford pizazz is now being used in behalf of this young company's zealous battle to become a recognized cultural force in the city of Los Angeles. This goal is still a dream, but Clifford and the dancers work hard, excited by the chance of creating a new ballet company.

In his role as artistic director of the company, Clifford has been building a group of polished dancers with sharp technique. While the local Los Angeles dance students slowly develop and feed into the company, he imports professionally trained dancers from New York City and other parts of the country. Clifford also welcomes the work of other choreographers, which is an important factor in developing a company. He has already collected a mixture of over seventy ballets, including works by

Balanchine, Petipa, Bournonville, Lenis, Dolin, himself, and others. And the dancers, led by Johnna Kirkland, show an adaptability and willingness to dance anything, anywhere, at any time.

As the Los Angeles Ballet Company's main resident choreographer, Clifford is prolific, daring, knowledgeable, and open to both growth and experimentation. He has an eye for pattern and for what the dancers can do. There's no question that he can take a piece of music and turn out a competent dance. Still, Clifford has yet to stop long enough or go deep enough to pull out a thematic focus that imbues his work with the magic of a personal sensibility. This, of course, is the ultimate mystery of individual talent because it goes beyond the craft. Clifford, himself, is aware of this aspect of the art of choreography from his years as a dancer with the New York City Ballet.

John Clifford not only danced with Balanchine's New York City Ballet Company, but he choreographed for the company and worked very closely with "Mr. B.," his heroic, model figure. I think it's important to understand that Balanchine's technical and conceptual innovations have influenced many young, contemporary choreographers, including Clifford. To be influenced doesn't mean to copy blindly or imitate Balanchine's work, but the basic ideas that Clifford and his Los Angeles Ballet Company are now working with descend directly from George Balanchine's inventive view of the classical balletic vocabulary and the way to exhibit that vocabulary on stage in a theatrical form.

From its first days in the Italian and French royal courts, it has been the nature of the classical ballet to blossom at different times in different cultures. Each renaissance adds an expanded image derived from older roots, but revitalizing the art. Balanchine, working within this tradition, pared classical dancing to a sleek quickness, which, in a sense, reflects modern American culture. In this process, he developed dancers that are referred to as "Balanchine dancers" and ballets that are labeled "Balanchine ballets." The dancers usually have long legs and a small head. Of even greater importance is the fact that a Balanchine dancer can move fast, is extremely sensitive to musical nuances, and has the ability to pass through movement without settling into postures and grand preparations. It is this last quality which is so special and so contemporary, yet the untrained eye cannot usually appreciate the subtle shifts of weight and the extraordinarily complex patterns that emerge from a Balanchine work. Balanchine ballets are without plotted stories, have little or no scenery, and use sophisticated music. Balanchine also choreographs story ballets, however, such as *Coppelia* and *Nutcracker*, that use elaborate costumes and sets, and ballets with popular music, like *Who Cares*, set to the music of George Gershwin. But the sparse, elegant poetry of pure dancing without elaborate visual or plot support is Balanchine's special theatrical image, and describes a "Balanchine ballet."

It is this heritage of Balanchine's innovative approach that John Clifford and the dancers of the Los Angeles Ballet Company have brought to Los Angeles. At present, the company is housed in a one-story, concrete building in downtown Los Angeles. Inside, behind a series of haphazard offices is a large room with the open randomness of an airplane hangar. A dance floor set on a raised platform takes up most of this large space. Baroque plastering embellishes the ceiling, mirrors cover the partitioning wall, and a piano, portable ballet barres, and boxes of costumes add to the dishevelled, temporary look of a space in transition. The dancers ignore the inconveniences and keep dancing. They want the Los Angeles Ballet to be on a par with the best companies in the country, so they take class, they rehearse, they work hard, and they don't complain. The question now is whether Clifford and this young company will thrive, mature, and develop as they grow. The future as it unravels, holds the answer, but the effort must be applauded.

The Young Eliot Feld

It keeps changing shape and if I defined it, I'd be stuck with it.

AT TWENTY-SIX, ELIOT FELD was a daring young man who had skimmed the surface of the established ballet world only to land on the rocky shore of his own talent. When I interviewed him for a WBAI program back in 1969, his American Ballet Company was about to make its American debut at the Brooklyn Academy of Music. Born the preceding year, with Eliot as its choreographer/director, the youthful company of eighteen dancers had already made a successful first showing at the Festival of Two Worlds in Spoleto, Italy. With the upcoming performances, most New Yorkers, including myself, would have a first look at this emerging company; it was an opportunity awaited in the dance world with both curiosity and bated breath.

Just two years earlier, Eliot Feld had made a blazing choreographic debut, *Harbinger* [1967], with the American Ballet Theatre Company, but instead of developing his talents within this major company, he did one more ballet for them, *At Midnight* [1967], and then left. This was both a controversial step and a very curious one, for in leaving American Ballet Theatre, Eliot was giving up one of a choreographer's most precious resources, the availability of trained dancers to dance out choreographic ideas. In addition, he was defying the established pattern of power in the classical ballet world with his decision to go it alone and establish his own company, rather than fit into a niche within the hierarchical order of the parent company's traditional structure.

The large American ballet companies, like the New York City Ballet and American Ballet Theatre, are patterned after the European national companies that, in turn, evolved out of the old feudal social structure. In a sense, these large artistic organizations are miniature kingdoms whose internal hierarchical structure reflects ballet's origins in the sixteenth-, seventeenth-, and eighteenth-century royal courts of Europe. The democratic attitudes of today's twentieth-century world have mitigated the rigidness of the early court-subsidized ballet companies, but traditions have a way of suffusing the thinking and order of the way things are done; in ballet, an aristocratic, authoritative heritage has lingered on. This tradition helps in ordering an unusually large collection of artistic personalities and creative energies. In effect, however, the ballet company does function with a belief that the "king's" wishes are law, and anyone associated with a traditional ballet company can proceed with his or her own artistic work only after approval has been given from the one or two people at the top. Like a royal court, the ballet company revolves around an artistic, but autocratic power, and all creative impulses emanate from that point.

The dancers, too, are part of this courtly tradition, and an individual's development from an entry-level corps member to soloist to star follows a prescribed pattern that has been set in harmony with the aesthetic standards of each company. But, as in everything involving strict rules, there is always the exception, and an unusually gifted, charismatic dancer will be pushed ahead of others in order to utilize both the dancer's special gifts and box-office appeal.

Eliot Feld, with two outstanding ballets choreographed by him in just one year, was an exceptional talent, only he wanted something that couldn't be given; the freedom to turn American Ballet Theatre's artistic views in what Eliot considered a more forward-looking direction. Challenging the authority of the company in this way could not work. He would be allowed to play a role as one of the choreographers whose work would be produced and danced by the company, but he could not control the overall aesthetic decision-making process. Whether he was right or wrong in his beliefs did not matter, he was out of step in reaching so quickly for a place beyond his own position in the ordered tradition. The power lay at the top of the court, not with him, and the answer was "No."

Eliot, young, talented, and headstrong, felt hampered by such a confining policy. It seemed as though tradition in the guise of leadership was stopping him just as he was starting. Coincidentally, Eliot's personal ambitions, which had led to his disagreement with the company's policy of relying on nineteenth-century romantic ballets and proven but dated twentieth-century revivals had the accidental consequence of placing him within another of ballet's ongoing traditions.

Since 1760, when Noverre, in his treatise *Lettres Sur La Danse*, pleaded for more humanistic, less artificial, ballets, there has been an historic pattern of dynamic tension between the ideal of a harmonious, meaningful dance and an exaggerated reliance on technical, acrobatic virtuosity. Often, the two approaches to theatrical dance exist at the same time in the work of different choreographers and legendary dancers, but essentially the classical ballet had tended to be dominated by either one or the other of these two aesthetic ideas. In fact, American Ballet Theatre itself was founded during a resurgence here of the ideal of making ballet a more contemporary, more meaningful experience for twentieth-century audiences. Over the years, however, the company has drifted towards the box-office aesthetics of gala programming and virtuosic exhibition, and so Eliot Feld, with his challenge, carried forward Noverre's centuries-old torch to rekindle American Ballet Theatre's original flames.

Still young, still ambitious, but his earlier reputation of a brazen young lad left behind. Eliot Feld (Photo: Newsday)

Eliot, determined to pursue his ideas about dance and not be bound by tradition, formed his own independent dance group, the American Ballet Company. By defining his artistic principles through rebellion against the existing order, Eliot placed himself, consciously or unconsciously, in another dance tradition—that of the American modern dance. Primarily an American art form of the twentieth century, modern dance has developed with the ebb and flow of individual dancer/choreographers' careers. Starting with Ruth St. Denis and Ted Shawn, these individuals have developed their own schools and founded companies to dance out their artistic visions. Working with small companies and limited budgets, modern dancers have not been burdened by the huge super-structure of dancers, musicians, and designers that make up the large ballet companies, and so feel less pressure to compromise their artistic standards to meet budgetary commitments. Theirs is a less popular form of dance than classical ballet, however, and with limited financial support available, they survive on belief and determination, focusing their art on the true nature of dance— the exploration of movement as it relates to the human experience.

Eliot, familiar with modern dance technique and ideas since childhood, fell naturally into this independent modern dance mold when he formed both his own company and his own school. But his youth and his relative inexperience as a choreographer made the formation of his American Ballet Company a feat comparable to the god Zeus's, when he caused his daughter, Athena, to emerge full-grown from his head. After the premiere of *Harbinger*, Feld was hailed as America's most gifted ballet choreographer, but it is one thing for your work to be part of a larger, mixed program of ballets, and quite something else to form and shape a company of dancers to perform a whole evening of your own ballets. And so it was no wonder that the dance world was waiting to see if Eliot's promising talent would equal his ambition, arrogance, and guts.

That first Brooklyn season constituted an acceptance of Feld's company, if not exactly an overwhelming success for it. The American Ballet Company was a young company and it expressed young ideas. *Harbinger*, the first ballet that Eliot had made for American Ballet Theatre and now revived for his own company, became, unintentionally, the company's signature piece. The lone opening figure posed between a huge, billowing backdrop seemed to symbolize the unresolved youthful emotions that appeared in various guises in different ballets of that season, while the ballet's explosive, hurtling choreography reflected the strong, youthful energy which Eliot knew how to channel into exciting movement. But in *At Midnight*, Feld's second ballet, a solitary young man stands outside of events he observes. Many questions of mood and statement were left unanswered by that season, but what was certain was the evidence of Eliot's mature control of his craft.

The most outstanding of his new ballets was *Intermezzo*, a lovely dance set to the music of Brahms. With breathtaking lifts and impeccable musicality, it revealed Eliot's inventive mind and his talent for subduing the classical technique to the needs of his work. Of the three other ballets in the company's new repertoire, *Meadowlark*, to music of Haydn, was the sunniest in spirit and seemed sure to remain in the future repertoire. It was first set by Feld on the Winnipeg Ballet Company of Canada in the period shortly after he left American Ballet Theatre. *Pagan Spring*, a variation on the primeval theme of awakening and set to music of Bartók, was not wholly successful, and *Cortège Burlesque* was a lightly satirical pas de deux. In addition, Eliot wisely complemented his own work with two ballets by Herbert Ross (*Los Caprichos* and *The Maids*), one by Donald McKayle (*Games*), and a revival of Michael Fokine's *Carnival*.

The company itself, composed primarily of teenage dancers, was refreshing but still a little unpolished in its performing skills. Somehow, the company's overall style—because of its youth, because of Eliot's use of movements evolving out of emotions and gestures, and because of its directness—fell midway between the dancing in a Broadway show and that of a classical ballet company. An improbable span? Perhaps, but one reflecting Eliot's own dance career, as he himself had gone from dancing in Pearl Lang's modern dance company, to the Broadway theatre, with *West Side Story* and other shows, and then finally to classical ballet at American Ballet Theatre.

At the end of his first season, no one knew what the future would hold for Eliot Feld and his ballet company. At his best, Eliot turned out well-crafted, fluid dances of dramatic gesture and poetic musicality with an undercurrent of anguished emotion. At his worst, he produced dances that suffered from slickness and silliness. It was evident there would be a future, however; Eliot was too talented and too single-minded to admit of any other possibility.

During the next three seasons, he turned out six new ballets—*Theatre, Romance, The Gods Amused, A Poem Forgotten, The Consort*, and *Early Songs*—before his American Ballet Company was disbanded due to insufficient funding. Having one's own dance company was a bit more complicated than simply churning out ballets for the dancers to dance, and certainly bearing that pressure alone was not easy.

One of the difficulties leading to the disbanding of Eliot's first company was the problem of finding a house of suitable size to perform in. The Brooklyn Academy of Music is a large old opera house, and the American Ballet Company needed time to develop a large, faithful following to fill those thousand seats night after night. Another problem was Eliot's use of a live orchestra, which makes an invaluable contribution to the dance experience but makes the production costs prohibitive.

After his company folded, Eliot spent some time working as a free-lance choreographer, but he missed working with a group of his own dancers. In 1973, however, the Rockefeller Foundation came to Eliot Feld's rescue with a large grant. With that money and an offer from Joseph Papp of the

New York Shakespeare Festival to use the Newman Theatre in the Public Theatre Complex at cost, Eliot went ahead once more and formed another company, the Feld Ballet.

Matured by his first experience, Eliot was cautious this time; for example, he used taped music instead of a live orchestra. The opening season, in June 1974, was a portent of future successes. The small house, with just 300 seats, was appropriate to the intimacy of the choreography, and the company, expanded to twenty-three, was more polished than the first company had been. Since the 1974 season, Eliot's following has continued to grow, and the critical response to the Feld Ballet has been encouraging. The company has toured through Mexico and South America, as well as across the United States, gaining both exposure and experience in these tours. As of this writing (1979), Eliot has created twenty-nine ballets, and though this work forms the base of the company's repertoire, from time to time guest choreographers are invited to set works on the company. Recent years have seen the acquisition of a loft for rehearsal and teaching; a school, called the New Ballet School, has been established; and an imaginative teaching program involving children from New York City's public schools has been initiated, both as a community service and as a way of discovering new talent. In January 1978, the Original Ballets Foundation, the administrative wing of the Feld Ballet, purchased an old movie theatre for conversion into a dance house. At thirty-five, Eliot Feld is still young and still ambitious, but he has been battered about enough, and created enough choreographic works so that his earlier reputation for being a brazen young lad has been shed and left behind—outgrown.

What remains as an identifying force is the overall aesthetic direction of the Feld Ballet, which has unwound in a direct line from those early Brooklyn performances of the American Ballet Company. Eliot is still an excellent craftsman, using dramatic gesture as an integral motivating substructure for his seamless choreography. He obviously has a sense of fun and an intelligent, roving mind. In some of his recent works, *The Real McCoy* (1974), *La Vida* (1978), and *Half-Time* (1978), he seems intent on playing with different cultural images: a movie-created figure of the debonaire man-about-town in *The Real McCoy*; Mexican life in *La Vida*; American "razz-ma-tazz" in *Half-Time*. These works are lightly programmatic and have moments of sheer delight, but there is a tendency for Eliot to deny the poetic potential of earlier works like *At Midnight* or *Intermezzo* and to skirt any real depth of feeling. It's understandable that as Eliot Feld grows and changes, so will his work, and whatever is true of his work today, the opposite might be true five years from now. But it is easy to imagine that Eliot's musicality and ability to blend gesture and movement will always be evident in his choreography, but that the way he uses these gifts to project his feelings about a piece of music, a place, or an idea will change. It is to be hoped that as he continues to develop, Eliot will allow the substructure of dramatic talent that bubbles like a spring in all his work to emerge in ballets revealing his full emotional power and wit.

But I've jumped way ahead of myself into the future, which is now. Back in 1969, Eliot Feld had the nerve to form his own company, the American Ballet Company. He had a very strong belief in himself, but he had no more idea of what the future would bring than I when we had the following conversation the year after that first season at the Brooklyn Academy of Music.

e.r. *You're both founder and chief choreographer of the American Ballet Company, which had its American debut last year at the Brooklyn Academy of Music. I say American debut because I believe you first appeared at a European festival.*

e.f. Yes, we performed at the Festival of Two Worlds at Spoleto, Italy, Gian Carlo Menotti's festival.

e.r. *How did you form your company?*

e.f. Well, it's convoluted. We knew we had an invitation from Gian Carlo to perform at the Festival of Two Worlds. With that in mind, I spoke to Harvey Lichtenstein [director of the Brooklyn Academy of Music] about starting a company in Brooklyn. One thing kind of led to the other and before we went to Spoleto, we knew we would be a resident company at the Academy of Music.

e.r. *But were you the one who suggested that you become the resident company at Brooklyn?*

e.f. I danced with Harvey Lichtenstein in Pearl Lang's Company when I was eleven and he was a little older. Then at different dance functions, awards, and things, I would meet him. I had left Ballet Theatre and I knew a short time after I left that I wanted to form a company because it was the only way I could do what I wanted to do. I don't know who brought it up, but it kind of happened through conversations that he knew I was interested and he was interested in building the dance program at the Academy.

e.r. *Does having a permanent performing space and season help you in forming plans for your company?*

e.f. Yes. It helps us in the sense that we know that we have two New York seasons a year, which otherwise we wouldn't know we had. Also that those seasons are subsidized to a large extent by the Academy. It also has helped to give us a kind of institutional base, which is very impressive, and understandably so, to many foundations. So in that sense it has helped us raise money. And just the use of the stage—at least when it's available—helps our rehearsals.

e.r. *Does the Academy give you a certain amount of money for the performances or is it based on what the tickets bring in?*

e.f. So far it's been a certain amount of money and that certain amount of money varies according to the financial conditions of the Academy, which also has its own financial problems; it works at a deficit.

e.r. *But does it help you to know that when you do a new work that work will be shown to an audience?*

e.f. Not only with an audience in a theatre, but with an orchestra, and with advertising, and in a fine dance theatre. It's a very fine dance theatre.

e.r. *How large a company do you have?*

e.f. I think we're eighteen at the moment, which is about the same size as when we started. I think we were sixteen when we started last year and we're eighteen now.

e.r. *What is it that you have in mind when you say you formed your own company because you wanted to do what you wanted to do?*

e.f. I can't really explain what it is that I have in mind because I'm really not sure. But, for instance, I was in American Ballet Theatre and I was just one choreographer among many. The Company had many varied interests and intentions and that's very valid for them, but I have my own dance aesthetic and I'm interested in expressing it. It's just more than each ballet that I do, one at a time. It has to do with a total attitude towards dance theatre. I'm interested in making a dance theatre and I feel that I have the ability to make a dance theatre that's never been made before. I say that without being competitive about it; without saying it's better than this or better than that. I have my own statement to make and I felt that I needed a situation that permitted me to make that statement without being interfered with.

e.r. *So that it could grow over the years?*

e.f. Yes, which is why I can't really tell what it is because it keeps changing. It keeps changing shape and if I defined it, I'd be stuck with it. I don't want to be stuck with it, I want to let it grow and see what happens.

1979

e.r. *It's incredibly hard to believe, but it's been ten years since you were getting ready for that season at the Brooklyn Academy of Music. Since then, you've choreographed thirty ballets and, though your first company, The American Ballet Company, didn't work out, you formed another one, the Feld Ballet, which is fulfilling your original dream. In these past years, you've also worked with ballet companies in Canada, Denmark, and Sweden. You've been busy.*

e.f. Always. I've always done a lot, working with my own company or with one of the large ballet companies. But there are limitations working with the large companies. There are only so many rehearsal hours available to any one choreographer. With my own company, the dancers are focused on my work and really, that's what it's all about.

e.r. *What would you say was the most important aspect of all that's happened to you in these last years?*

e.r. I think the only thing that you can learn is to rely on your own instincts. There's nothing else to rely on or to learn. You can't depend on critical evaluation or audience response because sometimes the work you do is in favor with the critics and the audience; sometimes you're out of favor. The only thing is to stay independent, for as long as you're independent you have a chance to change and grow and evolve.

e.r. *That's easier said than done. It requires a lot of strength and courage to stay independent.*

e.f. But the alternatives are so bleak.

e.r. *Taking over the old Elgin movie house to convert into a dance theatre is part of staying independent, then?*

e.f. There's a problem of getting medium-size houses for medium-size dance companies.

e.r. *What's happening with that plan? The architect's model looks like an ideal theatre.*

e.f. We're now raising money to remodel. Hopefully, it will come in soon so we can get busy on changing the Elgin over to a dance house. We had hoped to have a season while we were raising the money to renovate, but we purchased it for less than the asking price and the owners didn't let us make a thorough inspection. When the theatre was turned over to us and we took a good look, we found that the condition of the house was so bad that we couldn't use it at all until it's been remodeled.

e.r. *And it's worth all the problems, headaches, and pressure of raising money and doing the remodeling?*

e.r. It will be a home for other dance companies as well as the Feld Ballet. We're not the only company in New York to face this problem. In the City, there are the large, beautiful, expensive opera houses, and there are the Broadway theatres and the lofts. There is no in-between and we're trying to deal with the problem. The opera houses and the Broadway houses are too big and expensive for our budget, and we don't really think we belong in a loft situation. So, hopefully, the money will come in and we'll have a dance theatre for ourselves and other companies.

e.r. *I have a feeling that you react to composers the way I respond to authors that I like. That is, when I like someone's work, I read everything, or just about everything that person has written. Am I right? Do you go right through a composer's work?*

e.f. Do you mean, listen to all of Aaron Copeland and then choreograph to it? No, I don't work that way.

e.r. *Your choice of music is so varied and you're such a musical choreographer, that I raised the question. There does seem to be a connec-*

tion, almost a translation of music into dance in your work. For example, to the Copeland music reflecting Latin America, [El Salon Mexico], you've choreographed La Vida *and* Danzon Cubano, *which also reflect in movement, style, and costume, the same images of Latin America as the music.*

e.f.   I don't consciously try and get inside a composer and translate the music into dance that way. In effect, it's the music that finds me and the dance comes out. When I hear certain music, I want to dance it out. It's a question of whether I feel it physically. It's absolutely necessary to me that the music has this feeling of dancing; only then do I start a piece. At the moment I'm working on a new ballet to a piece of music by Hindemith. I heard this piece of his and it got to me. I've been listening to it and now I'm working with it, section by section.

e.r.   *And would you like to talk about this new piece you're working on?*

e.f.   Not now.

e.r.   *With both modern dance and classical ballet in your background, why or how did you choose to work within the classical framework?*

e.f.   I don't make that distinction between ballet and modern dance. Dance is dance to me. But a lot of people would say, in fact, that I'm not working in the idiom of the classical ballet.

e.r.   *Your connection between feeling and movement is closer to a modern dance aesthetic. Generalizations always smudge the particular, but there is a thrust to what I would call meaningful movement in your choreography.*

e.f.   I think the feeling of weight in movement is an innovative, important contribution of modern dance. The nineteenth-century balletic ideal of movement was lightness and airiness. I try and explore space in both ways. I don't like to limit my movement to either one ideal or the other. I don't block out an airy life that defies gravity, but I'm not afraid of playing with the power of gravity and the effect it has on the body's movements. Also, the American jazz rhythms, which are very complex, have affected today's dance.

e.r.   *Your vocabulary is basically that of the classical ballet, and you do use pointe work.*

e.f.   Not everything is on pointe. In essence what I consider classical is the purity of line and the clarity of rhythm. The basic structure of the classical built on a clear, almost geometric alignment of the body in terms of the relationship of the parts to the whole. I work with that essential concept, at least as a starting point. The possibilities of movement involving those principles are limitless, and, of course, very beautiful.

e.r.   *Does it take a long time to choreograph a ballet?*

A movie image of the debonair man-about-town. Eliot Feld in The Real McCoy *(Photo: Lois Greenfield)*

e.f.   I get very involved when I'm choreographing.

e.r.   *I realize. It's practically been impossible to schedule this interview.*

e.f.   Nothing else really exists for me when I'm choreographing. I can't get involved in anything else and I don't like giving any time or thought to anything but the piece I'm working on because it's so preoccupying. Sometimes it takes three weeks to do a piece; sometimes it takes a year and a half.

e.r.   *There's no regular pattern?*

e.f.   No; there aren't any rules. I've worked on something for five years and then not used it. But that's fine because the material has become part of my body and it will come out in a different form or in another way. There's a double edge to choreographing in the sense that there's both an inevitability in the way a ballet tumbles toward an end, and yet I never really feel like a ballet is over.

e.r.   *Your latest ballet,* Papillon, *was favorably reviewed at its premiere at Artpark in upstate New York. I'm sorry I missed seeing it.*

e.f.   I'm sorry too.

e.r.   *Did you work from the music or were you influenced by the tragic story of Taglioni's pupil, who died after her tutu caught fire during a rehearsal for a ballet to this same music?*

e.f.   The Offenbach music lasts about two-and-a-half hours. I listened to the record, which is about an hour and twenty minutes. I read the back of the record jacket and that had the story of Taglioni and her earlier ballet, which happened about one hundred years ago. But the idea of butterflies, I felt, is not dissimilar to all the sylphs and nymphs that appear in the nineteenth-century romantic ballets. There's a hero in my ballet who runs after butterflies and the poetic ideal of the man who tries to catch butterflies has a lot in common with James [a character in *La Sylphide*], who falls in love with a sylph. It's that notion of the romantic search for perfection in an imperfect world. It's a little Byronic. Obviously, that ideal isn't going to be so total in our twentieth-century world. Even the dream isn't going to be so innocently romantic. In today's atmosphere there's going to be an edge of irony on that romantic ideal.

e.r.   *And that's what* Papillon *is about?*

e.f.   When you're talking about it, but that's not it. Dancing is something that can't be described. Dancing or a ballet is really what it looks like. The audience sees exactly what the dancers are trying to communicate.

Eliot Feld has said that during his high-school years, he would come home from a day in school, play ball, eat dinner, go dance in a Broadway show, come home, and do his homework. He was an unusual teenager. To maintain that kind of a schedule, he had to be bright, disciplined, and exceptionally ambitious—words that still describe Eliot.

Substitute an unending schedule of choreographing, rehearsing, and performing for the boyhood high-school routine and it becomes evident that Eliot functions today with the same intense drive. That formidable concentration and energy of his youth is now focused completely onto his ballets and his company. In the process of updating the old Brooklyn interview, I learned that he was so engrossed in finishing and rehearsing a new ballet, *Papillon*, that he had little time available for anything else. This didn't surprise me, as the creative process is all-absorbing. And in addition, Eliot has the burden and responsibility of directing his own ballet company. Nevertheless, I was amazed that when he finishes one ballet, he immediately starts a new one. Right after the first performance of *Papillon*, he began choreographing a new work to the music of Paul Hindemith.

The only possible explanation for such a concentrated routine is that an all-consuming passion together with the necessity of building a repertoire demands an intense commitment. Eliot has had this single-minded commitment for practically all of his life, so for him, the intensity is a natural way of living. This image of unremitting hard work belies Eliot's earlier rebellious image, which emerged not only from his actions and other people's observations, but from his own comments about his work: "I didn't like being a peasant in *Giselle*. There I was, wearing orange tights and a straw hat and some grapes on my back. I thought, what am I doing here? I thought of myself as some angry young man, and here I was, dressed in this outfit."

Eliot has often stated that he knows what he is about even if he'd rather not use words to describe what he prefers his choreography to communicate. When he does give in to verbal explanations, he talks in an off-hand, relaxed manner, in a voice tempered by the flat, even tones of a native New Yorker. He is sure and direct in what he says, with an ever-ready wit that is sharp and streetwise. It pops out unexpectedly in conversation. "Eliot," I said, "I don't know if our talk will be long enough."

"Make it up," came Eliot's instant reply, "everyone does."

"But, I don't feel right doing it," I answered, awkwardly.

"You're ethical?" Eliot retorted, throwing out his answer like a low curve ball. "You won't get anywhere that way," he added.

It was half true, half bait; the kind of remark that leads to a verbal ping-pong game, but Eliot had been too quick for me and I started to answer in a serious vein, "Where do I want to go? I'll tell you about this book . . ." I swung at the ball instead of stepping back, and the game was over.

That same quickness and love of irony surfaces in Eliot's ballets. It gives *The Real McCoy* a stylish flirtation with the image of movie idols like Fred Astaire, who dance dreamily away with the girl of a thousand dreams; and in *Half-Time*, it sustains a quirky, fun look at our culturally inflated view of sports. Often, this urge to mock, like a fast repartee, bounces into Eliot's choreography through a gesture or visual image, coloring a serious intention with a second, ironic look.

And Eliot's quick reflexes sustain his plans—for his company, his studio-school, his theatre, and his program for teaching ballet to school children in the deprived neighborhoods of New York City. Eliot says he's not being altruistic; that he's running the free tuition program because he's looking for talent that can be developed. Having been on the receiving end of one of his curve balls, I think this is another one of his half-truths, but coming from a different direction, thrown out as dust to distract attention from that side of him that is not ironic, but humanistic and caring.

Initially subsidized by the Feld Ballet, the New Ballet School's innovative program depends on grants and financial appeals to stay in operation. That adds up to a lot more work than would running an open school associated with the Feld Ballet, which owns three custom designed studios, and could easily accommodate a large, money-making school. Such a school could support the company financially instead of adding to its problems as the present program does. But Eliot and his associates, instead of following the traditional open-school path, have chosen the challenge of establishing the first free ballet training program for children attending the public schools in the disadvantaged sections of New York City. Eliot explains, "There must be millions of children in the schools who undoubtedly have talent, but no exposure." The Feld Ballet is going to fill that gap, but there's got to be an underlying attitude or feeling behind that decision that says: Wait a minute, someone give these kids a chance.

The children are auditioned in their own public schools by Eliot and his assistants. They look, Eliot candidly says, "for the children's natural facilities: for coordination, for a feeling of musicality, for a light in their eyes, and for the enthusiasm that shows they want to dance." The children who are chosen in the auditions are bussed in to the Feld Studio's New Ballet School in Manhattan one day a week for a half a day. They are given shorts, T-shirts, and ballet slippers; then the lessons begin. Though delighted, the youngsters at first hide their pleasure beneath giggles, groans, and shyness. Gradually, they ease into the routine, the discipline, and the French names for the new steps they are learning. Returning to their home schools, the children show their classmates some of the steps and exercises they are learning; the children who have not been chosen for the ballet lessons seem to be more curious than envious of the ones who take the classes.

Enough progress has been made during the first year of the program for one of the children to say, "If I were a king, I would like to stay in ballet because I like it." And Eliot has been able to fulfill the pragmatic side of the venture by using nine little girls in his new *Papillon* ballet. However altruistic or practical its inception and motivation, the full effect of the program and the idealism of the project is understood and appreciated by one of the mothers whose child was chosen to participate. "You have said to all these children, 'It's possible, reach for the stars.'"

"Eliot," I ask, "doesn't that make you feel proud?" Eliot takes a puff on his cigarette, and in spite of his casual, nonchalant interviewing attitude, a glint of enthusiasm bubbles up. "The purpose of this school is to make dancers, but for many of these kids, just to be in a place like this, around people working hard at what they love, and with a pianist playing music . . . well, that will make an impression."

Index